Massively Open

How Massive Open Online
Courses Changed the World

Jonan Donaldson
Eliane Agra
Mohammed Alshammari
Andrew Bailey
Daniel Bowdoin
Meghan Kendle
Lauren Nixon
Lisa Wressell

This work is licensed under a Creative Commons Attribution-NonCommercial-NoDerivs 3.0 Unported License.

Jonan Donaldson, Eliane Agra, Mohammed Alshammari, Andrew Bailey, Daniel Bowdoin, Meghan Kendle, Lauren Nixon, Lisa Wressell

ISBN-13: 978-1482775334

LCCN: 2013906891

CONTENTS

Acknowledgments   i

Foreword   iii

   Introduction: 1
   What's Up With MOOCs?

1   Disrupting Higher Education   21

2   Education through Interaction   47

3   Taking Learning Into Our Own Hands   63

4   A Wealth of Free Knowledge   79

5   Untangling from the Hype   91

6   Climbing the Ladder of Academic Integrity   101

7   Is The Gold Star Worth It?   113

8   Wrapping up the MOOCs   119

Bibliography   127

Index   145

ACKNOWLEDGMENTS

The authors would like to thank Dr. Mary Bucy for her leadership, extensive support and fostering of innovations in the Master of Science in Education: Information Technology program at Western Oregon University.

Foreword

Dr. Mary Bucy

For the past several years, the Master of Science in Education: Information Technology program at Western Oregon University has offered a course called Big Thinkers, in which students read best-selling and classic books about issues surrounding advances in educational technologies. As students develop their technology skills in the program, they also begin to think about the consequences, both intended and unintended, that these new technologies have in our world. Each term students explore a different topic, ranging from technology's influence on our minds, to its impact on our evolving education system, to the role it plays in a democratic society. With the introduction of Web 2.0, or the Read/Write Web, we have evolved from a society of knowledge consumers to one of active contributors. In response to this shift, we decided to experiment with flipping the model of the Big Thinkers course to allow our students to be knowledge producers by publishing their work.

In the first 12 months since they hit the world stage, MOOCs have taken the education world by storm. Many articles and opinion pieces have been written, but no books are yet on the market. Our Big Thinkers class, under the guidance of instructor Jonan Donaldson, decided to explore the literature around the MOOC phenomenon and to compile their findings into a published work. They wanted to innovate by using the many collaborative tools now available online, and so, rather than writing and compiling individual book chapters, they worked together, in real time, to write and edit this book as a whole.

The following pages are the results of their efforts, collaboratively written and published through the use of the very educational technologies they are studying. The book is published under a Creative Commons license in hopes that it will become a part of the larger conversation around open education, educational technologies, and the impacts they will have on our society.

Dr. Mary Bucy
Coordinator, MSEd Information Technology
Associate Professor, Western Oregon University

· INTRODUCTION ·

WHAT'S UP WITH MOOCS?

Internet technologies have transformed our world in a powerful way. They have changed the way we communicate. They have allowed us to become producers of content rather than being passive consumers. They have caused massive changes in our relationship with the entertainment industry. They have had a drastic impact on journalism and media, and have had powerful influences on government and politics. However, they have had only superficial influences on the educational system. Until now...

Massive Open Online Courses (MOOC) have entered the educational landscape and popular imagination at an unprecedented rate. By the time the first MOOC appeared, online education had been evolving slowly for nearly two decades. Within one year of the launch of the first course with truly massive enrollment, several million students had enrolled in MOOCs. On the surface, they appear to be just another type of online course, but there are many differences between a MOOC and a traditional online course. When a student enrolls in a traditional online course, the student is charged tuition, earns college credit, and the online class size is usually limited to about twenty to thirty students. Class size in traditional online classes is limited so the student can interact with the instructor. A MOOC, however, is almost always free, not for college credit, and class size is unlimited (Pappano, 2012).

According to Sean Michael Morris and Jesse Stommel from Hybrid Pedagogy (A Digital Journal of Teaching and Technology), a MOOC "is not a thing. A MOOC is a strategy. What we say about MOOCs cannot possibly contain their drama, banality, incessancy and proliferation. The MOOC is a variant beast - placental, emergent, alienating, enveloping, sometimes thriving, sometimes dead, sometimes reborn" (Stommel & Morris, 2012). Essentially, they have explained that MOOCs elude a simple definition because MOOCs are constantly changing and evolving by the instructors, institutions, and companies which create MOOCs and the students who learn from MOOCs.

MOOCs were first introduced in 2008 through a University of Manitoba course called Connectivism and Connective Knowledge and the term was coined by Canadian University of Prince Edward Island's Dave Cormier (Popenici & Kerr, 2013).

MASSIVELY OPEN

Widespread international interest in MOOCs began in 2011 when Stanford Professor Sebastian Thrun's course "Introduction to Artificial Intelligence" was offered in MOOC format through Stanford University. Anyone could take the class as long as they had an internet connection. Over 160,000 people enrolled in the free online class (Vollmer, 2012). Thrun's course was a catalyst for launching Udacity. The three most well known MOOC providers by the middle of 2012 were the organizations Coursera and Udacity, and edX, a not-for-profit company (Reich, 2012).

Both educators and policy makers have wanted to provide quality higher education at low cost universally. Before the advent of MOOCs, many people in developing countries did not have access to higher education, and economically disadvantaged students in developed nations were at an extreme disadvantage. Today, anyone who has access to the internet can be a student at no cost. Online learning allows people all over the world to learn nearly any subject for college credit, professional development, or personal interest. However, there is a lot about online learning and MOOCs we do not know. This book is an attempt to examine both the positive and negative aspects of MOOCs.

The new millennium brought increased saturation of internet technologies in society. Web 2.0 and social media tools are inextricably interwoven into the fabric of our lives, and to an ever increasing degree, into our learning experiences. Digital natives find the traditional modes of education to be stifling and foreign.

The sudden arrival of MOOCs on the educational landscape, along with the accompanying media storm, hit educational professionals in a visceral way. Some had great foreboding, and others had newfound hope in the face of what they felt was an increasingly hopeless environment. At both extremes can be found those who believe that MOOCs could be a disruptive innovation with consequences to education analogous to that of the personal computer on the world of mainframe computers.

Innovations with lasting impact can either be sustaining innovations or disruptive innovations. Sustaining innovations are those which improve upon existing technologies and practices. Online education has so far proven to be a sustaining innovation since it has served to help traditional educational institutions reach students who were previously not able to be physically present in the classroom. It was not, as some hoped, the magic bullet which would transform the educational system because it has generally been implemented by traditional institutions as an extension of traditional educational practices. In order for an innovation to be disruptive to the educational landscape, it would have to provide an easy-to-use and cheap alternative. To become a disruptive innovation, there is no requirement that the innovation be of better quality. Disruptive innovations of the past usually start as lower quality alternatives, but improvements over time usually make these innovations far superior quality to that which it disrupted. The MOOC has brought about renewed hope as well as fear because it isn't an innovation which necessarily supports the traditional educational system, but rather threatens to provide an easily available and low cost alternative to the traditional institutions to which there are often many barriers, including cost, location, and entrance criteria.

Although all the elements are in place for MOOCs to become the disruptive innovation which transforms educational systems around the world, there is also no guarantee that it will be anything but a flash in the pan. In the past there have been innovations which appeared to be on the verge of becoming disruptive innovations, but failed for a number of reasons. The most common reason a potentially disruptive innovation fails to become disruptive is quality. Although initial quality is low, if the quality does not soon surpass that of the original system, it is likely that it will not become disruptive and in most cases will fade into obscurity. Another reason they fail is that the preexisting system finds a way to disarm the threat posed by the innovation by turning it into a sustaining innovation for the old system.

There are those who are expending enormous amounts of money and energy trying to make sure the MOOC has a shot at becoming a disruptive innovation to a system that desperately needs disrupting. Some believe that our educational system has become a dysfunctional monstrosity which is producing increasingly worse levels of academic achievement while increasing in cost at an exponential rate.

Simultaneously there are others who are spending just as much money and energy trying to make sure it does not become a disruptive innovation. Some have a stake in the traditional system, from educational institution faculty and management to textbook publishers, testing services, and government officials.

The fate of MOOCs is unclear and will be affected by a complex interaction of numerous factors. However, the most powerful factor may turn out to be a population fed up with enormous costs of the status quo. If they turn en masse to MOOCs as an alternative to the educational system, the demand will provide incentive for MOOC producers to increase the quality, availability, number and type of MOOC offerings.

Availability is clearly the most enticing feature of the MOOC. In most educational institutions, a student must go through the process of becoming an admitted student before enrolling in classes. Some allow students who are not formally enrolled to take classes, especially their online classes. However, this also requires an application process which often takes up to a few months. MOOCs have the advantage of being available to students at a moment's notice without an application process. Enrollment is usually as simple as signing up for an account and registering for a course, a process which takes only a few minutes.

Then there is the problem of cost. Some countries have systems, ranging from kindergarten to doctoral studies, which provide education at minimal or no cost to students at all levels. Unfortunately, this is not the case in most countries. Educational institutions have no choice but to charge tuition. If MOOCs continue to increase in popularity, if the number of MOOC offerings continues to increase at all academic levels, and if they become systematized in a way that students can either earn credit or complete certificates and degrees, it is conceivable that traditional educational institutions will be unable to compete, except in the rare case where prestige of a degree from the institution makes it worth the cost.

The issue of quality, although still questioned by many, is rapidly becoming a non-issue due to the research into best practices in design of online learning, resulting in quality of instruction and academic achievement equalling, or in some cases surpassing, that of traditional face-to-face instruction not only in MOOCs, but also in their cousin, the fully online class.

Another issue relating to quality is that MOOCs have several inherent advantages over other traditional forms of instruction. The first of these advantages is that by nature MOOCs allow for gathering massive amounts of data as students are learning, thus making it easy to optimize the learning experience and in some cases even individualize instructional content and learning activities. There is no classroom teacher in the world who can tailor instruction to each individual student in order to give them learning experiences optimized for the student's own needs in terms of pace, content delivery methods, types of practice activities, and additional instruction in areas of weakness. However, with MOOCs the technology exists to make individualization and course optimization possible.

A system designed to automatically adjust learning to each individual student is an enticing aspect of the MOOC. Another related aspect is that of student choice in learning. In a traditional educational institution, students may be presented with several options in terms of which instructor they wish to study a particular class. Often there are no choices available. As the range of MOOCs continues to grow, the number of choices available will grow. This will introduce into the picture something like a market economy because students will be able to make more decisions concerning the courses they take. They already have the option of taking courses offered by professors from the highest-ranked institutions in the world.

Individualization as an automated process is an intriguing possibility. Another more common form of individualization is that of learning through the choices students are allowed to make. Students are often presented with a variety of learning activities for each module. They may be required to select a few of their prefered activities. There have also been experiments with gamifying MOOC courses. This involves using a badge system based on the idea of quests in massive multiplayer online role-playing games. To demonstrate mastery of a certain learning objective, students may have a choice of many activities for which they can earn a badge. Completion of a course is based on earning badges which demonstrate mastery of each learning objective in the course - not on completing every assignment in the course.

Individualization of learning is a possibility in a MOOC environment, but it is not an aspect of every MOOC. What is an aspect of every MOOC, however, is that each student is required to participate. Passive learning is not an option. Active learning is at the core of every MOOC design. Students cannot proceed to the next module of learning until they have mastered the previous learning, usually with a variety of learning activities being required. Therefore, even if instruction is not individualized, active learning is demanded - something that is not an essential part of many traditional classroom courses.

Another inherent advantage is the social nature of the tool. Digital natives have grown up in a connected world. Social media and the "read/write" nature of the web have become part of how they learn. The traditional classroom isolates students. It expects each student to do their own work, so much so that what is normally considered collaboration would in such classrooms be called cheating or plagiarism. Therefore, the traditional educational system is unnatural and uncomfortable for the digital native. MOOCs, which are fully online, have spread globally and integrate social media tools. They are therefore more comfortable for the digital native. They are a better match for their social learning proclivities.

Educational professionals have increasingly come to the conclusion that human beings, being social creatures by nature, are naturally predisposed to learn through social interaction. There are even those who philosophize that learning is inseparable from social interaction. In other words, learning at its essential core is a social process. If people learn best through social activities, what better platform than a learning system based to a large extent on what has been most effective in social media platforms?

In a traditional classroom, often the social aspect is minimized as the teacher delivers content and the students are expected to listen, read, watch, and practice. There are an increasing number of educators who turn their classrooms into dynamic social situations based on research into best practices in project-based learning and collaborative learning. MOOCs have the advantage of allowing connections between a potential pool of hundreds of thousands of students rather than the typical classroom of forty students. In such a massive online social environment, students can make connection with others with diverse backgrounds - a grandmother in India, a ballet dancer in Poland, a construction worker in America, an elementary school student in Tanzania, and a bank teller in Japan - thus increasing the possibility of greater depth of discussion brought about by bringing various points of view into the conversation.

In a traditional classroom it is usually possible for a student to sit quietly at the back of the room. In online education, including MOOC classes, students are expected to interact with their peers. Many online classes are designed in such a way that students will not be able to proceed to the next learning module until they have engaged in meaningful discussions, shared their own work, and given feedback to classmates. These interactions can occur using build-in tools such as forums, blogs, wikis, chats, and shared virtual whiteboards. Whether in synchronous or asynchronous modes, these tools can be set up to require students to interact with peers in pairs or small groups with high levels of social interaction. In other words, there is greater "distance" in traditional classrooms than in online classes.

The internet made an amazing range of possibilities available for social interaction. It also increased the wealth of information available to everyone. In the past, many types of information were difficult to access. The internet was originally envisioned and designed as democratic and a free place for free flow of information. The motto of the early pioneers was "information wants to be free." However, the first generation internet became a one-way information delivery system. The vast majority of users used the internet to find information, not to publish their own information. The tools by which one could publish information were simply too hard to use. To create a website one would have to learn HTML and find a place to host the pages they created. In the second generation internet, also called web 2.0, easy-to-use tools are freely available which make it possible for ordinary people to become creators and publishers.

This massive shift must not be underestimated. Throughout human history there has always been a small minority who were information content creators and publishers. The rest of us were consumers of information. This was the case with books, newspapers, magazines, television, movies, and the early internet. Today the consumers have become the producers. Along with this shift comes an ever-increasing availability of information on all topics available. Wikipedia is just one example. It is only natural, then, that a wealth of freely available information would someday be accompanied by a wealth of freely available educational possibilities. The MOOC may be one such venue, although it might evolve into another form with another name.

The internet provides greater access to a variety of kinds of information never before available to such a large number of people. For example, music streaming services allow people to listen to songs for free, whereas in the past they would have had to purchase the album. The same is true of many books and journal articles, and YouTube allows those who in the past couldn't afford cable television to now watch their favorite music videos. The range of possibilities was limited in the past for those who could not afford to buy things such as cable television service, CDs or books. These barriers have been eroded. The MOOC may provide an opportunity to do for education what other services have done for media.

MOOCs hold enormous potential. However, there are serious problems to consider. One of the first issues raised is that the quality of education in MOOCs is not always what it could be. There have been MOOCs which were simply recorded videos of classroom lectures put online, where students took multiple-choice midterm and final exams. Such course designs and the resulting learning achievements have proven to be dismal failures. Online learning requires a different kind of course design than does a classroom course. Online courses must include a variety of content delivery methods, a variety of learning activities, a wealth of activities for practicing new learning, and a significant amount of peer interaction. The best MOOCs do indeed include these necessary aspects, but not all MOOCs do. In fact, it is possible that the majority of MOOCs fail to implement best practices in online course design.

Traditional educational systems around the world have produced populations in which the majority are not self-motivated learners. Students depend on the teacher to tell them what they should learn, how they should learn it, when they should learn it, and how they will know when they have learned "enough" to get a passing grade. They are not taught to develop self-directedness in their learning. This is a major problem with MOOCs, as well as all online education, which requires a much higher degree of self-directedness, motivation, and personal time management.

This reliance on the teacher to provide guidance, motivation, and time management is exacerbated by the problem of grading. Most students and teachers expect that assignments will be graded. This comes from the expectation in the traditional education system that teachers will evaluate students, rather than students being taught to continually self-evaluate their own mastery of learning. Students are taught to look to the teacher to tell them how they are doing, rather than knowing immediately how they are doing themselves. In a traditional class, each assignment is evaluated by the teacher, who will then record a grade which contributes to the course grade, and will also be given to the student. In a MOOC with over a hundred thousand students, it would be impossible for the instructor, or even a team of instructional assistants, to evaluate the work done by each student. The first way this problem is addressed is with machine grading. However, machine grading is only effective for tests with multiple-choice or true/false questions - obviously not an effective way to measure mastery of learning. Other MOOCs have attempted to use peer-grading systems, but the results are mixed at best.

Although the practice of grading, whether by the teacher, the student, or peers can be less than helpful or even harmful, the practice of giving useful feedback is unquestionably a necessary part of education. In a MOOC it will never be possible for students to get personal feedback from the instructor or other course facilitators. It will never be possible for computers to give an appropriate depth of feedback. This leaves only the possibility of feedback from peers, a practice that can be valuable when set up carefully, but can be quite problematic if not set up according to research-based best practices. Unfortunately, a haphazard approach to instruction for discussions and other forms of peer feedback can be a common occurrence in many online courses, including MOOCs.

Another difficulty inherent to the MOOC is that student readiness is ascertained only by the student. In a traditional educational setting, student readiness is determined through a range of measures such as prerequisites, grades in prior courses, and placement tests. None of these are part of the MOOC system, and therefore leave the ultimate decision up to each individual student. This could lead to students' self-placing into inappropriate levels. If students enroll in courses which are below their level they may become disinterested and decide to stop pursuing educational activities altogether rather than enrolling in courses at a more appropriate level. If students attempt to take a course beyond their level, they will likely become discouraged and give up.

If MOOCs are ever going to achieve respect and recognition on par with for-credit online courses with limited class sizes and direct instructor observation of all student work, they will need to eliminate the potential for cheating, plagiarism, and other forms of academic misconduct. In many online courses, assessments are proctored. Students are asked at the beginning of tests to turn on their webcams, hold up a picture ID demonstrating the students are who they claim to be, and show the proctor that there are no other people in the room and there are no devices such as cell-phones on the desk. During the test, the proctor watches everything the students do. The proctor can see the student's face through the webcam, and they can see everything appearing on the student's computer through a shared desktop. This is possible in classes with limited numbers of students, but when class sizes get into the thousands as is the case with MOOCs, proctoring is impossible. If MOOCs are not offered for credit there is little incentive to cheat. However, if MOOCs are offered for credit, the incentive to cheat becomes a serious problem.

Once students decide to cheat, doing so is much easier in MOOCs than in other kinds of online courses. In a credit-bearing course through a traditional educational institution a student can sign up for a specific course only once per term. In a MOOC, students can create multiple accounts, which would allow them to take tests multiple times until they get good scores. In a course with a limited class size, instructors get to know their students' writing styles, and can easily spot instances when students turn in work they didn't create themselves. Obviously, this would be impossible in a course with thousands of students.

Some MOOCs have offered special certificates to students who sign up for test proctoring for a fee. This can be quite unfair for students who are taking MOOCs due to financial difficulties. Perhaps a student in a developing nation whose family lives on a dollar or two a day has found a way to gain access to the internet and signs up for a MOOC. A twenty-five dollar proctoring fee may seem small to a student in a developed nation, but it could be an impossibility for others. If the noble goal of free education is extended to anyone in the world, it seems wrong to take that away by adding proctoring for a fee into the equation.

Millions of students have enrolled in MOOCs without the promise of college credit. They do so for many reasons, but the desire to learn appears to be front and foremost. The push to turn MOOCs into something different - courses in which students can earn college credit - could be interpreted as the first attempt by the established traditional educational institutions to eliminate the threat of MOOCs becoming the disruptive technology, which could potentially put them out of business. The alternative could be unthinkable to them. If left to follow one logical path, MOOCs will continue to evolve until totally free degrees become available to anyone in the world who wishes to pursue higher education. It is easy to imagine a startup becoming an accredited degree-granting institution and also able to continue offering high-quality free online courses to anyone who wishes to learn through non-traditional funding arrangements such as advertising and relationships with potential employers looking to scout the best and brightest from amongst the graduates. Perhaps funding could also come from non-governmental organizations where many hold the belief that educational opportunities is a human right which must not be subjected to financial barriers or market forces.

On the side of those who fear or dismiss MOOCs are those who argue that they are simply a natural continuation of a long-term process to discredit and disempower educators. Star educators are enlisted to create content and educational activities for MOOCs, and other educators might be pressured to "flip the classroom" - having students learn content from MOOCs as homework, and then in class use the education delivered by the star educator as the basis for their class discussions, activities, and assessments.

Another argument against MOOCs is that they are usually built by large teams of specialists, each with a unique skill set. For example, there might be several content experts to handle various learning outcomes, instructional designers trained in best practices in online course design, programmers skilled in creating artificial intelligence systems which analyze student behavior in real time in order to deliver individualized instruction, and a whole team of facilitators to facilitate online discussions. No classroom teacher could ever hope to deliver such complex learning environments. Therefore, even if MOOCs prove to be able to provide quality education, they put the whole profession of teaching in jeopardy.

Perhaps instead of the question being whether or not MOOCs can provide quality education, the question will become whether or not MOOCs should be allowed to compete with traditional education. Universities are rushing to join the MOOC bandwagon, perhaps not because they wish to increase quality of instruction, but because they wish to neutralize a potential threat to their very existence. How such conflicts play out will be fascinating.

Disruptive innovations have unintended consequences, both good and bad. If the MOOC turns out to be a disruptive innovation, we must carefully consider the repercussions and prepare for them. When the automobile first appeared on the scene there were many people who found it to be a fascinating and exciting innovation, while others found it to be a source of incredible irritation. What nobody foresaw, however, is that hundreds of millions of people have been killed in automobile accidents. Should we have made automobiles illegal a century ago? Is the convenience worth the cost? Although these are after-the-fact questions, there are always new questions we must seriously debate when new innovations arise. The MOOC is not going to kill anyone, but when potentially disruptive innovations arise we have a responsibility to do our best to understand where the innovation might take us, as well as the potential costs and benefits. This book is the beginning of a discussion we hope will enable educational professionals and other concerned individuals to help shape the future of education toward a more open, accessible, and effective model.

· CHAPTER ONE ·

DISRUPTING HIGHER EDUCATION

Since the turn of the new millennium, there has been a huge proliferation in interactive web 2.0 tools, access to high speed internet service, and students comfortable engaging online. This digital age has been described "as one of the recurring periods in world history when far-reaching changes in economics, culture, and technology raise basic questions about the production, preservation, and transmission of knowledge" (McNeely & Wolverton, 2008, p. 7). Today's teens are the first generation to have grown up with the influx of social media allowing them to feel at ease with conducting most of their social lives online. This indoctrination of online socialization has prepared these students to interact with their teachers and fellow students in ways older generations find hard to fathom (Harden, 2013). These digital natives require something more than the standardization of learning and linear transmission of information and knowledge that characterized the educational model of the industrial age.

With the sudden popularity of the MOOC, many educators and experts in the field are claiming this could be the disruptive innovation that will finally move higher education out of the industrial age educational paradigm and into a model that better serves the realities of the 21st century. The former U.S. Secretary of Education, William Bennett, has likened the MOOC movement to "an Athens-like renaissance" and John Hennessy, President of Stanford, compared it to a tsunami (Carr, 2012). This chapter discusses the factors that have led to a growing discontentment towards the system of higher education and how the MOOC, through continued improvement to big data and machine learning, can be the disruptive innovation that transforms the landscape of higher education and meets the learning needs of today's digital student.

A Need for Disruption

The rise of the MOOC has come at a time when the cost of higher education seems to have reached a tipping point. Over the past three decades there has been growing skepticism over the rising cost of a college education. The cost of higher education has increased fourfold leading to a an overall feeling that a college education is not attainable for most

(Pew Research, 2011). Today, the average cost of a four year degree (including room and board) stands at well over $100,000 (NCES, 2011). There are many factors contributing to the huge rise in cost including bigger and better facilities, recruiting "star" faculty for the ever growing demand for research, and a continuing decline in state support over the past four decades (Schejbal, 2013).

The cost of post secondary education has skyrocketed and the average household income has remained relatively flat, taking into account the rise in cost of living (DiSalvio, 2012). The disparity in the rising costs for education and stagnant wages has forced many families and students to take out loans to pay for college. This resulted in almost a quadrupling of student debt in less than a decade. In 2004, total student debt was around $260 billion and today that number is over $1 trillion (Cohn, 2012).

Despite these numbers, research has found that a majority of students still say their college education has been a good investment for their future (Pew Research, 2011). In addition, census data shows that the median annual difference in income between a college and high school graduate is nearly $20,000, equating to about $650,000 over the course of a work life. However, data shows that for youth today times are different. The rise of the MOOC is happening when the current economy is not able to support the growing influx of college graduates. A thirty eight percent increase in college graduates over the past decade and a struggling economy has lead to over half of all college graduates under the age of 25 being unemployed or underemployed (Weissmann, 2012).

When graduates are able to find a full time position, many times it is not a position in their field of study. Many recent graduates found the only jobs they could land were as servers, bartenders, cashiers or retail clerks (Associated Press, 2012). These positions were rarely the career opportunities that were promised to these hopeful graduates. They desperately took on an increasing amount of debt just to pay for the education they were told they so desperately needed in order to obtain a good paying job that would secure them a productive place in society.

The reality is that times are tougher for young adults. Nearly half of college graduates report that paying back their debt has made it harder to make ends meet. The Federal Reserve has reported that more than a quarter of student loan borrowers, of which there are thirty seven million, are behind on their payments (Pew Research, 2011 & DiSalvio, 2012). At the same time, by an almost 4 to 1 ratio, adults say it is harder for young adults to pay for college and to find jobs than it was just a generation ago (Pew Research, 2011).

A 2011 study by the Social Science Research Council (SSRC) showed that in their first two years of college, nearly half of all students failed to demonstrate any significant growth in "their ability to perform tasks requiring critical thinking, complex reasoning, and written communication as measured by the Collegiate Learning Assessment" (Arum, Roksa, & Cho, 2011). It is no wonder that nearly sixty percent of Americans believe there is a gap in value between what a student spends for a college education and what they actually receive from colleges and universities (Carr, 2012). Given the current condition of the economy and the college educational system, it is difficult to argue there is no need for drastic change.

The spirit behind much of the MOOC movement today is to allow anybody with an internet connection to access classes and courses for free with a trend to charge those who want accreditation a minimal fee. The MOOC approach to the distribution of knowledge and information has the potential to be the disruptive innovation that will not only lower the cost of higher education but also decrease student debt.

What is a Disruptive Innovation?

In his book, *Disrupting Class*, Harvard Business professor Clayton Christensen describes his disruptive innovation theory to explain how and why organizations struggle to adapt to particular kinds of innovation and predict how organizations can use innovation to succeed. Christensen maintains there are two types of innovations in any industry. First, there are sustaining innovations which simply are meant to improve product performance but do not upset the current market. An automobile that can go further on a tank of gas, a better screen resolution on a tablet, or a copier that can make copies quicker are all sustaining innovations. Now and then something different will come along that is not just an incremental step in improvement but actually transforms the industry. This new product is able to cause a disruption even though it is usually substandard compared to the existing technology. However, because it is more affordable and easier to use, the disruptive innovation creates a much larger pool of consumers by being able to reach those who were unable to use the technology previously (Christensen, 2011, p. 45-47). Over time, the disruptive innovation, through continuing product development, outperforms the old technology and new companies supplant old companies (Meyer, 2010).

Christensen relays the story of the personal computer (PC) as a classic disruptive innovation. Before the PC found its niche in the early 1980s, the dominant player in the computing industry was regarded as one of the premier companies in the world, Digital Equipment Corporation (DEC), the manufacturer of the minicomputer. Although smaller than its predecessor, the mainframe computer, (which took up an entire room), the minicomputer still cost over $200,000 and required an engineering degree to operate. This left DEC with a very small consumer base and plenty of room for potential market disruptors to appeal to those who had been left out of the market previously because of the high cost of entry. Apple, Inc. was one such disruptor who quickly gained market share with their inferior yet more affordable products. Apple's first PC model was originally marketed to children as a toy, so the expectation to be as powerful as the minicomputer did not apply. As Christensen points out, complete market disruption takes time to occur and initially the PC had little effect on DEC's growth or profits. However, in a decade's time, through frequent sustaining innovations from the new PC market and huge improvements in microprocessor technology, the PC could do the work that once required a mainframe or minicomputer. Needless to say, the entire world was virtually transformed by the PC. Everybody was better off except for the minicomputer industry, including DEC, which was non-existent by the beginning of the 1990s (Christensen, 2011, p. 48-50).

Past Innovative Disruption in Education

Walden University emerging technologies professor and futurist David Thornburg contends there have only been two technological innovations that have truly revolutionized education--the phonetic alphabet and the propagation of the mass-produced book in the 16th century--and suggest that mobile technology could become the third (Noonoo, 2013). The MOOC movement is poised to contend for the title, although it certainly is not the first time the education industry has claimed it was on the cusp of the next great innovation that would revolutionize education.

In the early 1900s, the modern postal system allowed colleges and universities to send their courses and lessons to anybody with a mailbox through what were known as correspondence courses. Colleges, extremely eager to enroll more students to create additional revenue streams, promised a more personalized learning experience, personal attention, and the ability to do the work at one's own convenience. The correspondence course phenomenon by 1920 had enrolled an astounding four times as many students than were enrolled on all college campuses. However, it did not take long before it was realized that the quality of instruction fell far short of what was promised and by the 1930s the revolution was dead (Carr, 2012).

It seems every generation has its own technology that claims to be the panacea for the ills that afflict the educational system. In the 1940s, the radio became popular, leading many people to believe it could be used beneficially as a means to transmit courses over the airwaves. Through a program called School of the Air (SOA), courses of study were designed for K-12 students that were integrated with their school curricula and were broadcast to listeners all over the United States. Although many held high hopes for the SOA movement, it never attracted more than ten percent of the student population (Bianchi, 2008). It was television's turn in the 1960s with President Johnson going so far as saying the solution to the teacher shortage of the time was through educational television. This failed exploration into the blending of technology and learning included an experiment in the 1960s where students in American Samoa received eighty percent of their content delivery via educational telecasts. It only took a few years before everyone, including students, realized their academic performance was slipping and the project was abandoned (Toyama, 2011).

The 1980s heralded in the PC revolution as millions of PCs started to make their way into people's homes. The first educational drill and practice programs were developed in 1981 for the PC, and by 1989 almost ninety percent of teachers thought the computer revolution was a "boon to education" (Associated Press, 1989). Although it supplanted the minicomputer and has made life unimaginably easier for billions of people around the globe, the PC has not transformed education like many thought it would. This history makes it easy to see the "repetitive cycle of technology in education that goes through hype, investment, poor integration, and lack of educational outcomes" that seems to plague the educational system (Toyama, 2011). Today's generation has certainly had their own share of potential technological saviors, starting with the internet in the late 1990s.

Innovative Online Learning

While Thornburg claims mobile devices to be the third innovative technology to revolutionize education, many other researchers and writers have dubbed a slew of potential innovations as the next disruption. These include wikis, blogs, social media, open source, RSS, Google, cloud computing, and virtual worlds (Meyer, 2010). None of these "fads", however, have lived up to the hype and they certainly have not transformed education. The question on some people's mind is, will MOOCs? Many agree with John Hennessy's appraisal that MOOCs replicate the disruptive innovations that have reshaped the global information, media and news industries, by shifting market power from the established players to parvenu start-ups and alternative providers (Boxall, 2012). More skeptical observers contend, on the other hand, that MOOCs will be more like modern versions of correspondence courses and point to the fact that MOOC providers do not have a sound business plan, therefore ignoring MOOCs as a threat to the establishment. However, Christensen (2011) points out that innovative ideas never pop out of the innovators' heads as full-fledged business plans. Rather, they are fragments of a plan (p. 75). No matter how you look at it, and although the business model is far from being perfected, there is no doubt investors see a huge marketing opportunity in having hundreds of thousands of captivated customers available to them. Because of the current market buzz surrounding MOOCs, the global MOOC market is estimated to be worth over $100 billion by 2015 (Boxall, 2012). This is an astounding figure considering the MOOC "heard around the world", Sebastian Thrun's graduate-level artificial intelligence course that enrolled 160,000 students from more than 190 countries, took place less than two years prior to that estimation.

Providing classes to students for free is an altruistic and commendable idea and could help curb rising costs and the debt crises. However, it is still unclear whether MOOCs can provide any guarantee of student learning. Some experts say online learning is just as effective if not more effective than face to face learning. Recent studies conducted by the U.S. Department of Education (DOE) have demonstrated that students in online conditions performed modestly better, on average, than those learning the same material through traditional face-to-face instruction (Means et al, 2012). The DOE results also indicate the use of videos or online quizzes do not contribute to a significant increase in learning, although they do give online students more control over their interactions with media along with providing opportunities to promote learner reflection can enhance the online experience (Means et al, 2010). These findings echo results by Dr. Katrina Meyer who found online learning to be more effective largely due to students spending more time on task, having more control over their learning and allowing for opportunities to reflect (Meyer, 2010).

On the other hand, other research shows students' motivation to learn is affected due to the nature of online learning and its tendency to lead to procrastination (Elvers, Polzella, & Graetz, 2003). For example, you may only need to check in once a week to submit an assignment, or during group discussions or video lectures online you may be simply logged in, yet working on something else simultaneously. However, in order to learn, students need to be actively engaged in the process of taking in information and, more importantly, processing that into a form that can then be verbalized and applied towards their own work. Students without those skills may have a difficult time adapting to this online learning environment. Christensen (2011) argues that while the data does show online learning may be more suitable to the highly motivated learner, the market is trending so that over time online learning will become more engaging so as to reach different types of learners (p. 100). When education is presented in a way that resonates with the way a student naturally learns, understanding comes easier and the learning can be intrinsically motivating (p. 27). This is why MOOCs are increasingly using innovative methodologies and new technologies to deliver content that promotes student engagement and processing.

Traditionally, online classes have largely been taped lectures, a format that is hardly conducive to student engagement. While some MOOCs also include taped videos of the professor talking, these talks are divided into short segments each of which are followed by exercises and quizzes, making MOOCs different. This format keeps the student more involved with the lesson and research has shown this type of feedback helps students' understand and retain the lesson better (Carr, 2012). Jeff Abernathy (2013), President of Alma College, has decided to use caution before jumping his school onto the MOOC bandwagon, arguing that today's students need more than moving the "sage from the stage" to the computer screen and adding a few quizzes to be engaged. While the MOOC movement may help reduce costs, what is most important is that we enhance our students' experience as we do so, not cheapen it (Abernathy, 2013). The fact is that the video lecture format is only one of many MOOC course designs. Many do not even have "lecture" content but rather readings, multimedia, interactive activities, discussion, and projects. MOOCs can change the way students learn by allowing them to explore and create through inquiry-based learning, project-based learning, challenge-based learning, like Carnegie Mellon's Open Learning Initiative, or game-based learning.

In the 2013 NMC Horizon Project Preview for Higher Education, game-based learning is highlighted as an effective learning tool which is quickly gaining popularity. Integrating games into the educational experience has proven to be beneficial in cognitive development and fostering of soft skills among learners, such as collaboration, communication, problem solving, and critical thinking (NMC, 2013). As MOOCs continue to transform the accessibility of information and courses, it will be important for course designers and teachers to look at how to motivate students towards completion of the courses and showing mastery. These pedagogical approaches could be looked at in higher education as a means to harness the power of MOOCs and bring students' learning to a higher level.

Machine Learning and Data Mining

Still, there are those who are not convinced that an online course can ever be as effective as taking a class face to face with an instructor. Online courses being taught by passionate, engaging professors can definitely provide opportunities for many people to learn. However, Greg Graham, instructor of writing at the University of Central Arkansas, asserts that what students need most is immediacy, something they feel a computer just cannot provide. What he means by immediacy is for students to receive customized instruction from teachers whom he regards as "artists using all their senses, including intuition, to learn what makes each student tick, and using every tool, including tactile and other forms of nonverbal communication, to reel the student in" (Graham, 2012). What Graham fails to see is the potential of large-scale data processing and machine learning or learning analytics, something Udacity co-founder Sebastian Thrun believes is the secret to developing engaging, student-centered course material (Carr, 2012).

Advances in analytical software has made it possible for computers to sift through large amounts of data that is collected throughout a course. Big data and learning analytics "refers to the interpretation of a wide range of data produced by and gathered on behalf of students to assess academic progress, predict future performance, and spot potential issues" (NMC, 2013). Currently, computers are able to track a student's choices and responses which affect the path a student might take in a course. David Kuntz, head of research at Knewton, a small company that specializes in adaptive learning, is in charge of developing online tutoring systems that are able to learn about a student's needs and learning styles and adapt the course based on the data collected. For example, answers to a quiz might provide the student with further information about a topic that has not been fully grasped or, after demonstrating mastery, take the student down a path introducing a new topic. Furthermore, the more data collected, the better the program becomes (Carr, 2012).

To accommodate for the fact that students learn in different ways, Kuntz predicts that soon the software will be able to automatically adapt the mode the material is presented to best fit the needs and learning style of each student. Basically, the computer is able to learn how the student learns by tracking where the student clicks, when s/he speeds up and slows down and is able to "anticipate their needs and deliver material in whatever medium promises to maximize their comprehension and retention" (Carr, 2012). The mode in which the material might be presented for a student could change for each stage of the course or may even change depending on the time of day. Whether the student learns best by reading text, watching a video, listening to a lecture, playing a game, or engaging in discussion, the software can meet the needs of each student.

Not too far off in the future, Kuntz predicts computers, through all the data mining and number crunching, will be able to provide an entire learning environment designed around the learning needs of the individual student. Despite the enthusiasm of Kuntz and other MOOC supporters for the advancement of analytical software, Timothy Burke, a history professor at Swarthmore College, is not convinced. From his perspective, it is not because of technical reasons distance education has typically fallen short of hype, but because the model has "deep philosophical problems" and he argues much like Professor Graham that, "the essence of a college education lies in the subtle interplay between students and teachers that cannot be simulated by machines, no matter how sophisticated the programming" (Carr, 2012). While this line of thinking feels good and takes us back to a simpler time and place, it fails to take into account the potentiality of large data collection.

Every variable and action a student makes during the course is tracked and cataloged. The massive amount of data collected from hundreds of thousands of students in thousands of courses will provide course developers and professors with information about what does and does not work for a course. One of Coursera's co-founders, Daphne Koller, points out that by collecting this amount of behavioral information in such minute detail about students, we can gain new insight and understanding about how people learn and master complex material (Carr, 2012). The possibilities that arise from these new insights are left to anybody's imagination.

A Changing Landscape

The MOOC movement has the potential to cause many changes to the higher education landscape. Will college campus enrollment decrease, programs of study close down at universities, or professors lose their jobs over this disruption in the realm of higher education? Some feel there will be change, but it will not be to the extent of putting colleges and teachers out of business. Today's college system has withstood the privatization of education and repeatedly shown itself superior to those for-profit schools in terms of job placement for graduates (Weissman, 2012). Research points to the fact that despite the massive growth in enrollment at for-profits colleges, public colleges have continued to increase enrollment as well (NCES, 2011). With the need for higher education in the job market today, more students are going back to school or attending college for the first time. However, these students cannot ignore the cost factor, and that is where the MOOC has found its niche. As courses continue to be offered online for free, students will continue to show interest in this mode of learning.

The future generation of college students have grown up in an environment that thrived on social communication through technology. The Educause Center for Applied Research reports that 70% of students say they learn best in a blended learning environment (Educause, 2012). Students want to be able to access content and information online. The MOOC model could serve as a launching point for a student's education that will lead them to classrooms on the college campus, much like the University of London which made the decision to offer MOOCs to catch the attention of individuals in developing countries. The hope is to use MOOCs as a potential recruitment tool to reach new students who then might want to take a course at a branch campus (Corbyn, 2012).

Another way universities may utilize MOOCs while at the same time providing for a richer, more engaging and efficient learning experience is to essentially flip the classroom. William Lawton, director of the Observatory on Borderless Higher Education, a UK-based research organization, envisions a scenario where many universities that provide relatively the same content, like an introductory course in economics, take advantage of a shared online platform like Coursera. The students would watch videos and explore course material on their computers in their homes and then gather at their separate campus classrooms or labs to discuss and explore the content more deeply (Carr, 2012). The 'flipped classroom model' is currently taking place on a relatively small number of courses, however Lawton warns, scaling up the model could have far-reaching implications (Corbyn, 2012).

Lloyd Anderson, former Provost and Senior Vice President for Academic Affairs of the University of Southern California, fears a much worse scenario for the traditional college campus due to the low cost and scalability of the MOOC. He argues that private competitors in education will utilize the blended learning and digital technologies available through the MOOC platform to separate or "unbundle" the teaching leg of the traditional college from the research and services legs of the university goals. This will lead to a shell of a university with little more than research professors, few students and a huge infrastructure that is seldom used (Hunt, 2011). While Anderson's forecasts may sound dire, he is not the only one that paints a bleak picture for the future of the college campus.

Jonathan Rees (2013), History Professor at the University of Colorado, equates this "debundling" to the power grab by managers of the industrial revolution in 'dispossessing the craftsmen of their accumulated skill and knowledge' by developing the specialization of tasks. He feels this debundling is the university administrators' way to do the same thing to the university professor. Bob Samuels echoes Rees' sentiments in his report of the UCLA Forum on High-Tech Higher Education. His main takeaway from the conference was how course delivery might be broken up into separate tasks like design, presentation and marketing. Samuels (2013) goes on to point out that a new business model has emerged in which institutions are repackaging great courses given by great professors, which they sell to other institutions of higher learning. This has many faculty members up in arms about what this means for their profession.

While taking a world history MOOC being taught by Professor Philip Zelikow of the University of Virginia, Rees saw the potential fallacy in this method. Rees explains that Professor Zelikow promised his UVA students that discussions would be held in groups on campus with no more than 60 students led by Zelikow himself. This is wonderful for those students actually able to make it to the UVA campus, but what happens to the students who are taking the class through Coursera out-of-state or even out of the country? At those other campuses, local faculty would lead the discussions based on the content from Zelikow's course. Rees dismisses the whole notion and warns,

> No self-respecting tenure-track historian would allow their content creation to be farmed out off campus because picking what they teach is what makes the job fun. Besides, as I've explained before, content knowledge is what makes Ph.D.s worth our salaries. Without it, we'd all be paid like high school teachers or even worse. Despite Zelikow's excellent intentions, this is how the debundling of the history professoriate begins. (2013)

In other words, Rees believes by allowing their work to be used by others, professors are robbing others in the profession of their joy and reason to work as well as risking the destruction of their very profession. Rees' biggest objection, however, is the belief that the private entities that take over the industry (venture capitalists), with little or no thought about what is best for the students, faculty or industry as a whole, will still get their profits whether they are able to provide an effective learning environment or not (Rees, 2013).

In a scathing rebuke of the entire MOOC movement, six faculty members from San Diego City College argue that the move by universities toward MOOCs devalues the position of professors, save a few "stars", relegating them to the position of simple "information delivery systems". They contend that professors' jobs will be to "become rope-makers for [their] own professional hangings" (Cost et al, 2013). In their opinion, MOOCs might help decrease the cost of higher education but it will not improve the quality. In fact, far from leveling the playing field for those less able to afford an elite education, they argue it will create a two-tiered system with those who are still able get the real face to face education from the prestigious universities and those who will have to settle for something "quick, cheap and easy" (Cost et al., 2013). Professor Graham points out the irony that a movement that is supposedly promoting an equalization of knowledge and information will actually, in his opinion, create a bigger gap between the "haves and the have-nots" (Graham, 2012).

However, the other side of the argument is that by dividing up the traditional tasks of the educator-- aided by advances in technology--learning can be made at once both more affordable and of a better quality. Most can agree, whether for or against MOOCs, that one of the biggest concerns yet to be solved is how to deliver content to a massive number of students but still keep the intimacy that is needed to form the meaningful relationships that are required in any successful learning environment.

Ted Curran (2013), instructional designer for Samuel Merritt University, argues it is the "personalized timely feedback and frequent interaction with the teacher" that is most important for a successful learning environment and not the quality of the lecture, textbook or use of technology. What seems to get missed in all the commotion is the idea that online learning and the dividing up of tasks will actually allow faculty the ability to give more personalized time to their students. For those faculty members who are worried about what their role will be in this shifting paradigm Dr. Katrina Meyer reminds them

> Someone needs to design the instruction, develop the self-help tools and course content, answer questions, and guide the confused. Someone still needs to establish the learning outcomes and design the assessments that will establish whether learning occurred. Someone still needs to address the needs of students who are not well-equipped to learn online: the unsure, the inexperienced, and the needy. Someone needs to help students learn how to learn, and how to do so online. Someone needs to be at the other end of the connection to offer support, a well-timed question, a reference, and a critique of what was done and how to do a better job next time. (2010)

There is obviously still plenty that needs to be done in order to develop an effective learning environment. The use of online technology simply allows educators to automate the less engaging activities like lecturing, exams, and grading and gives them the freedom to focus more of their attention on creating student choice based on student need and interest (Curran, 2013).

Instead of viewing this shift as a battle pitting live professors against learning management systems that track a student's every move, it is better to embrace the best of both worlds and work in tandem to create better educational outcomes. For anybody who has ever served as a teacher in a classroom, either in secondary or higher education, it is clear there is more to do in any one class than any one teacher can manage effectively. This can be seen in the fact that teachers are easily burnt out, a reflection of the 46% of educators who are out of the profession within their first five years (Curran, 2013). Instead of trying to do more with less, imagine what kind of learning environment could be created if courses were taught by a team of educators with diverse and complementary skills and strengths.

This type of design is something referred to as the disaggregated faculty model and has already been implemented in online, competency-based institutions with fanfare. Jodi Robison (2013), Director of Assessment at UniversityNow, claims a disaggregated faculty model is better because faculty are no longer overwhelmed by trying to do it all. There are many important roles to fill in this type of model. Some faculty members will collaborate with instructional designers and subject matter experts to design courses while others will be facilitators giving them the opportunity to work more closely with students. Still, others may choose to focus only on assessment and evaluation. One benefit of this model is that by separating the assessment role from the instructor role, any potential assessment bias from the educational experience will be removed. Robison (2013) argues, "such a design should build stronger confidence in the mastery level of the student because student performance will be judged based on what is demonstrated, independent of the student's engagement with the instructor". Moreover, a disaggregated faculty model allows students to establish a more developed learning network because the course design, facilitation and assessment are done by different members of the team. Most importantly, instead of trying to be all things to all students, educators can focus their time and attention on what they do and know best allowing them more time to give personal attention and feedback to students (Robison, 2013).

What Next?

The question must be asked whether or not the higher education system, as it is today, even needs to be saved at all. The traditional university was designed around the fact that students had to physically be in the same location as the professor in order to obtain the information required to learn and develop (Horowitz, 2013). Today, this model is no longer needed nor sustainable. Online learning has already proven itself to be as effective, if not more effective, than face to face education. With continued improvements to big data and machine learning, the future of online learning promises to move away from standardization and be more engaging and student-centric. This eliminates the necessity of physicality between student and professor. The skyrocketing tuition costs over the past thirty years and subsequent student debt bubble have rendered the system unsustainable. Because of this, NYU professor, Clay Shirky, argues "the possibility MOOCs hold out is that the educational parts of education can be 'unbundled' allowing for the educational opportunities to reach people who did not have them before" (Horowitz, 2013). MOOCs share this trait with other disruptive innovations as Clayton Christensen (2011) found in his research that "to succeed, disruptive technologies must be applied in applications where the alternative is nothing" (p. 74). In other words, if MOOCs are going to succeed in disrupting the traditional college system, MOOCs must be made available to those non-consumers who were denied market entry before.

The short history of the MOOC follows another storyline found to be similar of past disruptive innovations. Christensen (2011) explains, "like all disruptions, it first appears as a blip on the radar, and then, seemingly out of nowhere, the mainstream rapidly adopts it" (p. 91). The MOOC movement is clearly following this trajectory which has many concerned about how universities will adapt. Clay Shirky worries that if traditional universities do not act quickly they will lose out to the likes of Coursera, Udacity and other virtual schools just like the music industry failed to respond to Napster and lost the download industry (Bustillos, 2013). However, if the MOOC is to prove to be a true disruptive innovation, that is exactly what will need to happen. The aftermath left by the adoption of any disruptive innovation is one where new companies or institutions supplant the old ones, and old ways of doing things are replaced by newer, better and more efficient ways. The pace of growth and popularity of the MOOC along with the promised steady development of sustaining innovations has put the MOOC on course to be the disruptive innovation that will revolutionize not only the higher education system but the way the entire world learns and is educated. Perhaps, instead of asking if the higher education system can be saved, it might be better to ask, does it need to be saved?

· CHAPTER TWO ·
_____

EDUCATION THROUGH INTERACTION

As we begin to peel back the layers on the MOOC and what it brings to the realm of higher education, it is important to look at the capabilities that exist through learning in an open and massive environment. In this chapter, we will present adult brain-based and child development studies regarding learning, look at the rapidly changing model of communication in the world, and discuss the important role that interaction plays in education. Specifically, this chapter will discuss the role of online interaction as a process and means for learning.

Brain Research on Communication

Many studies have shown that the adult brain has the ability to continue to develop. In the neurosciences this is called plasticity, but in common language this is called learning. In a paper published in Proceedings of National Academy of Sciences, Veronica Kwok, Li-Hai Tan, and their colleagues at the University of Hong Kong, conclude that the adult human brain is, "…capable of new rapid growth when exposed to stimuli similar to what babies experience as they are learning…" (Yirka, 2011). Although adults learn through different mental processes than do children, their power to learn is just as great. However, for both children and adults learning is a social activity dependent to a large degree on the quality of interactions with other people.

A guide provided by the National Council for Curriculum and Assessment (NCCA), lists four strategies from which children learn through interaction. They are building relationships, facilitating, organizing, and directing (National Council for Curriculum and Assessment, n.d.). Each one of these strategies requires the child to interact with peers using multiple means of communication, in order to have their bests interests met. As you get older, the first aspect, building relationships, continues to increase in importance. Consider, for example, how a potential employer views new job candidates. No matter the questions or type of interview, one may assume that they will be judged on the basis of how they communicate and connect to the hiring panel.

Since MOOCs are based online and you may not know any of the other hundred thousand participants, you are thrust back into the early childhood role of having to start over in making new connections. Think about the networking aspects of MOOCs. You are taking a course that may or may not be along your lines of interest. Yet, you are still sure to have the opportunity to find and build relationships with others who do share your own interests. This is not always the case in a regular classroom. You come to class, occasionally have group discussions, and then go your way.

The second strategy is facilitation. "Children learn by being involved in making choices and decisions" (National Council for Curriculum and Assessment, n.d.). Online education brings the learner to the front of the room in terms of interaction. To complete any group tasks or projects, you need to interact and communicate with those you are working with. No more sitting in the back of the classroom, taking notes, and listening to the instructor and other students discuss the subject matter. You are forced to try to put your best foot forward, as your work and input is not just seen by the instructor, but is now evaluated by your peers. Not only will it be evaluated, but it will be discussed, tested, and altered. While this may lead you to change your initial decisions or choices on a matter, you will have learned through the process of interacting and collaborating with other students.

The last two ideas presented by the NCCA on

effective learning models deal with allowing the individual to organize and direct the situation and/or their environment. MOOCs can allow the learner to decide when and where they will be studying, plus with whom and how they complete the task. It is powerful for an individual to take that ownership of their learning and desire to receive new information and knowledge. The platforms in which MOOCs are built allow for a much greater degree of student self-directedness, while also providing a suite of tools for peer interaction.

Much of the new information and skills that we accumulate comes through the means of communicating with others, whether it be face-to-face, the media and news, or social interactions online. A study in 2012 which focused on the less discussed white matter portion of the brain reported that this part of the brain accounts for about 50% of the brain volume and serves as the communication network (Schlegel et al, 2012). So, half of our brain is dedicated to communication? How does this impact the thinking of educators when they put together a course? How the instruction is delivered and received must both be a focal point in the overall course design.

Research-based best practices in online course design suggest that anyone who is planning to implement an online course successfully should be putting primary focus on how they can effectively apply multiple modes of communication throughout the coursework and structure. This will allow the student to fully utilize that white matter portion of their brain, which in essence acts like a connection cable between the different processing centers of the brain. Once those connections start to form, the brain can further process the information. As more online courses are developed, the means through which communication is implemented will play an important role in the overall success of student achievement and learning.

Growth of Online Education

We are seeing a significant change in direction of communication and an increase in online and technological communication. As interaction and communication in society continues to rapidly adapt to new technology and changes in the tools we use, the ripple effects are being felt on a massive scale in the realm of higher education. Distance education from its inception has been marketed as a solution for adults whose occupational, social, and/or family commitments limit their ability to pursue educational goals (Lenoue & Eighmy, 2011).

In the decades since the 1970s, demand for distance programs has increased as the globalization of national economies creates a competitive atmosphere that drives people to become lifelong learners in order to be successful in the workplace (LeNoue & Eighmy, 2011). With career changes made along the way, adults naturally are looking to learn new skill sets. For many, heading back to a college campus is simply not realistic.

Much has been discussed about online education and how it impacts those taking it and the colleges who support and implement them. The statistics regarding the demand for online-courses are positive and show that online courses are increasing in popularity. Predictions have been made in the last few years that the growth of online education would begin to plateau and become stagnant. However, through an annual survey of 2,600 higher-education institutions in 2010, it was reported that the "highest-ever annual increase in online enrollment - more than 21 percent " had occurred (Kaya, 2010).

In 2009, colleges reported that "one million more students were enrolled in at least one web-based course, bringing the total number of online students to 5.6 million," up from the previous year's 17 percent increase (Kaya, 2010). An increase this size would indicate that online courses in higher education are becoming more popular and demanded by students. Could this be an indication that higher education is becoming more web-based with less in-class and face-to-face interaction?

The same survey found a 20 percent spike in the number of for-profit institutions stating that "online education is critical to their long-term strategies" (Kaya, 2010). It goes on to report that three-quarters of higher-education institutions say that online education is an integral part of their long-term plans, with for-profit institutions in the lead. Elaine Allen, associate professor of statistics and entrepreneurship at Babson College and co-director of the Babson Survey Research Group, suggests that the disproportionate increase in the for-profit sector may mean that online programs are becoming their 'bread and butter'. Colleges are telling themselves that "if we want to grow and have profits, we need to be in the online sector" (Kaya, 2010). In other words, consumers are creating a demand for online education which educational institutions are racing to fill.

Participation in online courses increased for the 10th year in a row, even as overall enrollment in higher education declined (Sheehy, 2013). With the 'newer' implementation of MOOCs in recent years, will this number continue to rise? It may be hard this early in the game to predict if MOOCs will continue to play a substantial role in the future of online education in a way that promotes access to higher education online, or if students will continue to stick with what they know--a 4-year collegiate program. However, 66 % of college administrators say that online education is the same as or better than face-to-face classes (Kaya, 2010).

Learning is Interactive

The buzz created around the implementation of MOOCs is one reason why the nature of this new learning model is catching the attention of everyone. The world we learn in is a world that thrives on social interaction and communication. Interaction is a critical factor in the quality of online learning and one in which everyone around has a voice (Heeyoung & Johnson, 2012). That voice wants to be heard.

Why not leverage this key aspect of human nature into a tool for increasing knowledge and skills that will be beneficial wherever we work, play, and rest? The learning model that the MOOC provides allows anyone to step back into the classroom and continue to develop their knowledge and skill sets. It is no secret that you continue to learn as you age, but for many the opportunities for fresh new information is harder to access once adulthood takes hold and endless other priorities arise.

We as a nation spend a lot of time online using social media. According to Nielsen's annual Social Media report, the U.S. spent 121 billion minutes on social media sites in just the month of July. Breaking that down into something we can comprehend, this equates to 230,060 years spent posting, tweeting and pinning. In addition, the survey found people spent more time on social network sites than any other category (Popkin, 2012). Simply stated, humans spend a significant amount of time interacting with others through the use of social media, smart phones, and tablets. If we want our students to be lifelong learners, then integrating learning with communication and networking with peers is important. Interaction in online learning environments has been found to have a close positive relationship with students' higher order thinking and cognitive learning outcomes (Heeyoung & Johnson, 2012). Research shows that these interactions have had positive relationships and positive outcomes, and positive changes in online learning formats such as MOOCs are emerging at an ever-increasing pace.

Humans want to achieve the most that they

possibly can. Maslow describes this in his influential book, *Motivation and Personality* (Maslow, 1970, p. 92). The ability to communicate to the masses via social media enables people to feel more self-accomplished due to reaching a larger population. While distance education has been used for many decades by students who can't afford to leave their job, home or families, we have seen a drastic increase in educational technologies such as communication tools, video conferencing, and multimedia content delivery tools. This has led to "an increasing body of literature in higher education [which] has discussed the need to use distance education for personnel preparation in a wide variety of curricular area" (Shik & Skellenger, 2012). MOOCs are rising to the challenge of meeting these needs by continuing to increase the number of subjects and content areas available through various online learning platforms.

Even as this book was being written, Coursera, which is one of the biggest start-up companies currently offering MOOCs by partnering with colleges around the world, announced that they had signed on an additional twenty-nine universities to deliver ninety-two more courses on their platform (Coursera, 2013). Announcements like this will continue to occur across the globe as colleges and probably more specifically, profit and non-profit companies, seek to provide a complete and rounded set of educational opportunities to all.

Last year saw a couple of different start-up companies jump at the chance to partner with elite universities to offer these massive open online courses to participants across the world. Coursera, being one of them, is stated by the New York Times to have a vibe similar to Facebook (Pappano, 2012). When you join, you create your profile page and update your personal information. From there, you can plan online or face to face meet-ups with others taking the same course. Networking and collaboration is an essential skill set in today's job market. In a world where the new resume is your online portfolio, blog, or website, it is important to show that you are connected to information and those from which you can glean new information. The ability for MOOCs to not only allow humans to learn new skills and information from anywhere, but to do so through a means that provides them with lasting connections, is an important player in the eyes of businesses and employers.

The MOOC movement takes advantage of the need in humans to share, and allows people to learn with others regarding a vast array of subject matter. Interestingly, the feeling among some is that the interaction provided in a MOOC is better than that found on a college campus. In a video interview discussing how businesses and employers may benefit from MOOCs, Chris Horton reflects back on his college days. He states that, "Most of my time spent was learning by myself" (Royer, 2012). This was during the time when he was going for his master's degree. Many college students may be able to relate. They go home and study or find a location in the campus library to quietly study alone. The social interaction we assume to be part of the college experience may be inaccurate. Horton's experience with MOOCs, on the other hand, provided interaction on a regular basis.

The ability we have to learn on the internet allows for many diverse interactive opportunities. Diversity can range from interactions with different age groups, cultures, gender, backgrounds, and experiences. These aspects of diversity will create a large pool of knowledge in education through interaction online. Since students do not all learn alike and have different styles of learning, the diversity allows them to choose the model that best fits what they need in order to receive the greatest benefit.

Interaction Brings About Collaboration

Students can use MOOCs to collaborate and learn from each other, learn from experts, peers from diverse cultures, and those from different backgrounds. Along with these assets come skills developed through online interaction such as "self-awareness, analytical thinking, leadership skills, team-building skills, flexibility, communication, creativity, problem solving, listening skills, and change-readiness", (Cleveland-Innes & Ally, 2012). The study conducted by Cleveland-Innes, et al, discusses the comparisons and contrasts of two different online delivery platforms and points out the overall benefit of learning through interactions online.

A benefit of online interaction is the accessibility and timing flexibility. Students have the ability to engage with one another and learn at their own pace, which is proven to be a benefit. Online classes seem to offer a more engaging and interaction-rich atmosphere between participants, (Cleveland-Innes & Ally, 2012). By supporting the use of interactive methods and multi-media materials, social software offers educators more ways to engage learners than any preceding educational technology (LeNoue & Eighmy, 2011). Through these new and innovative interactive methods and social software, the increase in online learning has become much more widespread. With the "new" technological advance in online learning, the increase could mean that we see a surge in 'attendees' at the higher education level that we have never seen, due to the fact that it is now accessible, affordable and 'in the home'.

Socialization is a big part of education through interaction. With the socialization process comes thinking, communication, motivation, and discipline. Students are forced to interact and learn with and from one another. As stated by Cleveland-Innes & Ally (2012), there is a learning benefit from learning through media because of the learning strategies implemented when using media. The skills required to learn through media differ from the skills needed in the physical classroom.

The article *A classification model for group-based learning* written by Strijbos, focuses on group based learning which involves education through interaction. Collaborative group work is proven to show increase in understanding and assists in the education learning process (Strijbos, 2000). Group work online is based on education through interaction and it forces each student to interact with one another and state their opinion. In online classes, students are freer to share their thoughts without having to worry about the responses and conflict that could happen with a face-to-face class. Furthermore, they are forced to participate because it affects their overall course grade, and often the system is set up in such a way that students are unable to see the next learning modules until they have satisfactorily completed the discussions, peer-feedback, or group project assignments. The whole interaction element of learning online has a totally different meaning from a face-to-face class. In a face-to-face class students are only required to be in class for the allotted time slot and interact willingly based on the teacher's requirements. Online, students are forced to interact and constantly log on to post work and provide responses to classmates.

Online Education: The New IEP?

Education is at a turning point where focus of learning is becoming more individualized, self-paced learning. Physical classrooms are based on a one size fits all method with instruction geared towards the whole class and not the individual needs and learning styles. With online education through MOOCs, the individual learning needs and styles are met and embraced through interactions of students with one another. Students learn and feed off of each other's strengths and weaknesses causing each one to learn through interaction with their peers.

EDUCATION THROUGH INTERACTION

As discussed by Abajian et al (2011), there are many ways to interact through MOOCs. Some of them are social networks, such as joining different groups online through Google hangouts which allows you to interact with each other with voice and video through the web. This creates a real life face-to-face classroom situation where students can feel a different level of connection with one another over the internet.

Another interaction method done through MOOCs is also mentioned by (Abajian et al, 2011), where students interact through course discussion threads. Here students are forced in some cases, depending on course requirements, to participate through forums for a grade in the course. A student posts his or her thoughts and then students reply with valuable questions and feedback. This process is done to create a back and forth conversation with peers, building the interaction time and expanding each one's knowledge and thinking on the topic. This forces students to form opinions and find ways to support them, which in turn forces them to really value their viewpoints and look at them from different perspectives.

To help value education through interaction, it is important to understand MOOCs and how they differ from a traditional face-to-face class. As mentioned by Masters (2013), one of the key aspects and benefits of MOOCs is the interaction given and received to gather and process the educational information. Furthermore, Masters discusses the importance of participation for education through interaction, because the lack of interaction would result in the lack of knowledge to learn from one another. Active participation is important and essential in online learning and the more interaction, the greater the value and knowledge gained by each student. The teacher is the supporting role in MOOCs, but the real learning is going on through interaction of the students with one another. Students are the ones exchanging ideas and concerns, as well as the questions and answers.

· CHAPTER THREE ·

TAKING LEARNING INTO OUR OWN HANDS

There are many benefits to Massive Open Online Courses. The key feature of distance education is that it takes place outside of the traditional classroom setting which is bound by space and time, therefore making it easier for anyone to take online classes.

There is an increasing body of research in favor of distance education, as well as many supportive articles on the positives of education online through MOOCs. The two main aspects discussed in this chapter will be distance learning through MOOCs, and the diversity that is created within that particular environment.

Given the fact that MOOCs offer classes to anyone in the world, students have the ability to interact and engage with one another, stay in one location, and are self-paced with their learning. It has been discussed that students learn best from each other, and the professor acts as the facilitator. Therefore, MOOCs can be among the best ways to learn and increase knowledge because they enable the student to take the lead role and the professor to support. As we move more toward independent and interest based education, the MOOC is a powerful tool because of its ability let you take online classes of your choice without going through a lengthy and difficult application, paying thousands of dollars, or being restricted by prerequisites. The world should embrace the idea of allowing more people to have access to education through the internet because of the positive aspects it brings.

Distance Education

When people think of online classes they often think that distance is no longer an issue, and with distance education it most likely isn't. In order to effectively educate a large group of students all at once, why not have an online course? This way a student no longer has to worry about travel time, travel expenses, or what modes of transportation are available. You don't necessarily need to leave your home, regardless of where the class is being taught. You just need a computer and internet connection.

According to Vollmer, a staff writer at creative commons, one goal of MOOCs is to serve a big group of people from all over the world with high quality education (2012). The "M" in the acronym MOOC refers to "massive", which implies that a great number of students can be enrolled in a single course at the same time (Rodriguez, 2012). Online education is able to accommodate more students simultaneously while virtually eliminating things like travel worries, lack of time due to family obligations, and time constraints due to work schedules.

MOOCs enhance learning by providing strong feelings of community, which can be easily lost when not physically entering a classroom. Community is extremely important in enhancing meaningful learning. A study by Liu, Magjuka, Bonk, and Lee found that teachers need to exude a sense of community to positively affect student satisfaction and reach the quality level needed from online learning (2007). MOOCs offer different ways of communicating and collaborating for students in that community to engage without "the fear of marginalization due to discrimination based on cultural or ethnic differences" (Young & Bruce, 2011). Since MOOCs are considered an open online environment that has countless interaction and communication between thousands of students, the sense of community is essential, and directly related. Students need to feel connected rather than isolated to involve themselves in the process of learning from an online course.

TAKING LEARNING INTO OUR OWN HANDS

How Education is Evolving

The face of education is changing. The idea of taking online courses and creating this new sense of community with the use of the World Wide Web is becoming the norm. Digital natives and digital immigrants alike are discovering the wide range of possibilities opening up through Internet technologies. Distance education is the new mode of schooling for an ever-increasing number of students, and there are plenty of positives surrounding it. There are new technologies and a corresponding body of research into best practices in teaching online, leading to a higher multitude of people able expand their knowledge. Until recently however, online education was available only to those who could afford to enroll in an educational institution. Not everyone had equal opportunities in terms of access to online education. Nonetheless, the number of students engaged in learning through online courses has risen steadily over the last two decades.

Crotty (2012), a research contributor states, "In the fall of 2010, 6.1 million students were enrolled in at least one online class". This research helps prove that online education is extremely useful in getting an education, and becoming more and more popular. Obviously more and more people are adapting to it and utilizing its possibilities. Universidad del Centro de Estudios Macroeconómicos de Argentina (UCEMA) professor Rodriguez (2012) states that when a student feels they have control over their learning, they are more inclined and motivated to learn. With distance education students can take control of their learning and mold it to what they want to focus on and how they want to increase their knowledge. Perhaps that is why it is becoming more widely accepted as a legitimate method of education. People can move toward personalizing their educational experience with online schooling.

Personal application that this type of learning brings can also shed positive light on other areas of life. It has been argued to be the best form of education in the world for adult learners by helping people learn and apply knowledge within the workplace, and expand their academic networks (Pappano, 2012). One can take an online class to help further their career while holding down a job and not have to worry about travel. Working and going to school has a whole new meaning that makes learning more manageable for students, as well as being more meaningful when the learning has real-life application in the immediate environment of the workplace.

Online Class Requirements

Online education encourages students to engage, collaborate, and self-direct more than a physical classroom requires (Crotty, 2012). Even though it would appear that one would spend more time on-task in an actual classroom, an online classroom demands more attention to detail. There is the need to constantly check online for posts and feedback, emails, online research, etc. It would be fair to say that distance education provides a new classroom feel for how learning can take place and how students actually take learning into their own hands.

True participation is required by the nature of the course design in most online courses which, although self-paced, demand student attention to master objectives and concepts before moving on. Students interact online with one another and with the material given to them. Teachers set goals for students to reach before allowing them to proceed to the next area of learning. It's a scaffolding process that needs a firm foundation. Setbacks are a given, but perseverance and persistence are key to success.

Students cannot be passive. Instead students are required to engage in content with frequent quizzes, online discussions, interactive activities, readings and assignments. Students become empowered learners as they tackle problems and acquire new sets of skills on their own with the assistance of their peers and guided by their instructor (Pratt, 2010). Because of the massive size of many MOOCs, courses depend heavily on student-to-student interaction as well as self-directed learning. In this format of learning students are able to process information at their own speed, thus allowing them to gain a greater depth of understanding. Furthermore, they are able to collaborate with other students in order to share their ideas and gain new insight from their diverse peers. One MOOC student mentioned that their experience learning in the MOOC environment was like having a tutor next to them (Pappano, 2012).

This feeling of having a tutor is created by having short video clips that can be watched multiple times, even slowing them down when needed. Unlike being in a crowded auditorium with limited view of the front, and taking notes, students in an online course have clear visuals and quizzes that check their understanding of the material.

Too often in physical classrooms, the quizzes and class discussions do not necessarily require the same amount of attention and participation. In actual classrooms there are students who answer questions for others because they know the answers. This can be a downfall for other students who do not get to answer questions. When this happens teachers aren't really assessing everyone's learning ability, nor are they helping students learn the skill of self-assessment. In an online distance class, you are required to understand the concept before moving on to the next lesson. Therefore each student is being assessed on what they know and understand. The teacher can then focus on re-teaching and modify any lessons that needs to be re-visited (Lionarakis, 2012). Most importantly, MOOCs usually have course designs centered around the idea of continual self-assessment.

With distance education there is a freedom that allows for communicating and conveying information by choice. There isn't that face-to-face accountability. Essentially, you have to want to do well. Rodriguez (2012) states that, "participation according to the students' learning goals, prior knowledge and skills, and common interests is what distance education is about". The model of traditional schooling was that teachers controlled what students would learn, when (and at what pace) they would learn it, and how they would learn it. Online education is closer to the ideals supported by all modern educational theory and research--the intrinsic motivation, self-directedness, and student-centeredness are the core of quality education. Although this may be difficult at first for some students, the end result is greater depth of learning.

The road of online schooling is an independent route and geared towards the individual student as opposed to the whole class. Furthermore, students are able to work together with like-minded people with similar interests and form study groups if needed--or they could chose to work with others of diverse interests. Study groups can be easier to form because you can use tools internal to the MOOC platforms such as discussion boards and instant messaging, or external tools like e-mail, Skype, Facebook, and many others, without having to leave your home.

Not only do MOOCs require dedication and hard work, they also provide the opportunity to have high quality education from high ranked schools and professors. It is a huge privilege to be taught by teachers from outstanding academic institutions from anywhere around the world. Typically, students have to pay a higher cost of tuition if they are to physically attend a class at an Ivy League school, for example, but with MOOCs they have access to the courses taught by professors from these schools.

This form of education brings learning and

social networking together as discussed by Pappano (2012). Social networking through online tools is the dominant form of communication in the digital age, with Facebook in the lead with over a billion users (AP, October 23, 2012). The internet is making it possible for students to interact with peers, experts, and mentors everywhere in the world.

Diversity

Many are fortunate to have taken a class with someone from another country or culture. Others, however, are not so lucky and lose the benefit of the different perspectives and opinions from those living in different parts of the world, as well as other elements that come along with online education. Diversity is a tool that helps mold education in different ways. What one may think is correct differs from others based upon each person's own culture and background.

The number of MOOCs and the number of participants have grown. In one MOOC provider alone, Coursera, the number of students grew from zero to over 3,110,00 in the first year of its existence (Coursera, 2013). Diversity is the result: "this massive size and the large number of international students greatly increases the diversity of classes" (Flicker, 2013). This means that, in a MOOC, students from all over the world from different cultural backgrounds, income levels, and geographic locations are actively engaged in content and sharing their knowledge, ideas, and opinions to the masses (Friedman, 2013). This massive size might be daunting at first for students, but once they enter into the content and discussions presented and formatted by the instructor, students are exposed to a variety of insights from their peers.

One MOOC student commented that the discussions they were a part of were so much more valuable and interesting than with people of similar geography and income level. This student was able to see the benefit of reading multiple points of view on a single topic which they might not be exposed to in a more confined and limited learning environment (Friedman, 2013). In the MOOC learning environment students are able to be a part of a learning community which shares a common goal and is enriched by the diversity of the community of learners.

Alanna Klapp (2013), in her article "MOOCs Open Doors for Diverse Student Body", points out that one of greatest benefits of a MOOC is the fact that it supports global diversity among students. Numerous universities share a common belief that diversity among students is essential to providing a quality education. According to Klapp, the 2U teaching program, as an example of MOOC, includes students from forty-five states and thirty-nine countries. She states, "diversity also enhances the online educational experience. The 2U technology platform allows students and professors to have a synchronous environment" (Klapp, 2013). Having this diversity in an online environment will enhance student discussions and critical thinking. Students learn more from those whose experiences, beliefs, and perspectives are different from their own.

Perhaps Vollmer (2012), New York Times writer, summarizes this point best by stating that it is the goal to have students from all over the globe become educated with a high standard of education. Some may be fortunate enough to have taken an online course from a notable professor. Better yet, some have been fortunate enough to even have been enrolled in the same course with someone from another country. This type of learning has enriched education simply by taking into account other world views. Diversity is a tool that helps mold the value of education. What one may think is important--or even correct--differs based upon each person's own culture and life experiences. It widens the concept of what "community" in learning truly is.

The Connectivism learning theory emphasizes the importance of a learning community in which a learner connects with information through connection with others. In this model a diversity of opinions leads to development of knowledge and skills (Kop & Hill, 2008). Connectivism learning theorists' view of diverse social interactions as important parts of the learning process is not new. Lev Vygotsky's research in cognitive development stressed the importance of social interactions (McLeod, 2007). Vygotsky's theory of Social Constructivism, one of the most influential theories in the field of education, views learning as the process by which learners are integrated into a knowledge community, and where they interact with others to help them organize and formulate new information and concepts ("Social Constructivism," n.d.). A world community of learners creates a much richer depth of possibility than does a localized community of learners.

In the MOOC environment, students have greater access to diverse social interactions because of the unlimited number of participants in the courses and the open enrollment policy which allows anyone of any age, geographical location, socio-economic background, or educational background to participate. This allows them to process information in different ways than may have been available in a smaller class size, as well as being presented with the opportunity to have a more in-depth understanding of a concept. By giving students these opportunities to communicate with a variety of learners, students are then able to process problems on their own.

Vygotsky viewed self-talk as an important process in learning since it allows students to work through complex problems by externalizing them as a form of self-guidance and self-direction. Self-talk is inextricably connected to social communication. Online forums in some ways bridge the gap between self-talk and social interaction because they are less threatening. Some students are more comfortable sharing their ideas and opinions in the online format of the MOOC. They like to take more of an "individualized" approach to learning, but still value others' opinions. This approach tends to give students the time they need to process what they have learned in order to develop more in-depth discussion of the topic. In addition, students have the opportunity to hear from a wide range of learners to add to their ideas. This opportunity allows for students to become exposed to new ideas and different ways of looking at things.

The individualized approach that comes with online learning is also ideal for students who are still learning English. According to Blackmon (2012), a researcher investigating online learning, online discussions allow students whose English is not their first language to take a more active role in debates. Online students can check their spelling and grammar before they post their thoughts and answers: "By communicating in an online, text-based format, students have an opportunity to check their vocabulary and sentence structure before posting to the board; this is a confidence booster for those who are new English speakers or those who are just unsure about word choice or syntax" Blackmon (2012). When people do decide to post their work online, others can chime in and help with not only their ideas, but also with language. The students still learning English can benefit from this without having to feel embarrassed or ridiculed. This makes distance education a collaborative effort.

MOOCs are an ideal environment for collaborative work which enhances critical thinking and supports Instructional-Design theory. "Online students can collaborate by sharing their individual perspectives, ideas, and personal experiences, thereby deepening their understanding with increasing higher order thinking and greater personal satisfaction" (Young & Bruce, 2011). Martha M. Snyder, a graduate school assistant professor in computing technology in education of Nova Southeastern University, wrote a paper entitled Instructional-design theory to guide the creation of online learning communities for adults to propose an instructional-design theory that supports a sense of community. She writes "the design theory elements of an instructional design theory for promoting online learning communities for adults include the goal, values, methods, and situations. These elements support an online learning community framework that is interactive, collaborative, and constructive" (Snyder, 2009). MOOCs are often have course designs centered around just such interactive, collaborative, and constructive learning activities.

Sharing Ideas

Sharing of ideas is enhanced with online communication through activities such as online discussions. This format also provides 21st century learning opportunities which better match the current technological environment. Palloff and Pratt (2010) note that "in everything from video games to the internet, our youth are coming to expect more active ways of seeking knowledge and entertainment". Therefore, education needs to provide active ways for students to construct knowledge using tools that are current and engaging (p.15). Online education has the ability to provide these active environments in which students can work with other students to construct knowledge while participating in engaging forms of learning.

· CHAPTER FOUR ·
───────────

A WEALTH OF FREE KNOWLEDGE

With the rising cost of higher education tuition at universities and colleges around the world, students are turning to other credible sources of education. The massive-open online free courses that are provided through places such as edX, Udacity and Coursera are filling demands which are not being addressed elsewhere.

When people think of continuing their education they often consider tuition costs, which can be a deciding factor in whether some continue their education or not. Students can scan many websites, flyers and brochures of different colleges to see what each has to offer and the overall costs of obtaining a degree at that location. Kolowich (2013), indicates the goal of the MOOC is to enroll students into courses with little to no tuition and

A WEALTH OF FREE KNOWLEDGE

increased support. Kolowich believes the solution is found by having students take courses through MOOCs. This is a risk free way to allow students to take an online course without having to worry about the pressures of having to drop out, the effect of their grades on their GPA, or the tuition cost of the course.

For the academic world, which isn't exactly known for being quick to embrace change, the past several months have been a whirlwind. Early this year, several well-known professors broke away from Stanford University to create two for-profit MOOC providers. In January, Udacity was born. Two months later came Coursera. Sebastian Thrun, a research professor of computer science whose free online course in artificial intelligence attracted 160,000 students worldwide, says he co-founded Udacity to develop a MOOC model in which students learn by solving problems, not by listening to a professor tell them how to solve them (Mangan, 2012).

Students are able to take university and college courses for free. Upon completion, some of these programs will offer a badge or certification stating that the student has completed the requirements. These can then be used to show employers the continued learning gain and knowledge expansion. Requirements in these courses may include quizzes and tests, but in most the bulk of the learning happens as students are able to develop their skills working with other students taking the same course through online discussions and locally-organized study groups. With MOOCs being available to anyone who has internet access, it is easy to see how one course can often include many thousands of students all across the world.

With the increase in students who have been enrolling in these classes, free online courses may provide another way to reduce cost and increase education access where budgets have been cut.

> Aside from offering evidence of job skills, free online courses could provide another strategy for reducing costs and increasing access in states where higher-education budgets have been cut ... a study released in July by Bain & Company, concludes that one third of the nation's colleges and universities are financially unsustainable. Expanding online classes is key to keeping costs down. (Mangan, 2012)

If expanding online classes is one of the emerging ideas in terms of keeping costs down in the United States, imagine what this could do worldwide and how it could benefit those who have no money to spend on higher education. Could this be the answer to help the world grow educationally? This is the often-stated goal of the MOOC paradigm: "The goal was and is laudable: to offer free, world-class education to anyone and everyone with internet access" (Snyder, 2012).

The idea of free online education is taking off around the world. It is becoming increasingly available and accessible for anyone who wishes to learn.

Open courseware – freely-accessible, internet-provider-cleared, comprehensive, university course materials – is already beginning to take off. Web-published course syllabi, reading lists with links to open access articles, course and lecture notes, video/audio lectures and audio-synched slideshows, together with essay assignments, problem sets, past exam papers and full-text readings, are now being used by self-learners, existing students, and young entrepreneurs worldwide (Pollak, 2008).

These free college courses are built by many of the top colleges and universities in the world. Some of the MOOC providers have over 2.5 million students worldwide enrolled in their free courses from top college and university professors. Research conducted by Zahn (2013) states "Maybe you're not quite sure what college you want to go to. The wealth of MOOCs available allows you to sample some of the faculty and course offerings at some of the nation's most elite college and universities. Wouldn't it be nice to be certain you'll enjoy your classes before you spend time applying and spend money on tuition?" With tuition costs not being a factor, people are more inclined to enroll in online classes to expand their knowledge because they have nothing to lose and much to gain.

UC Berkeley last October launched its own YouTube page, with full lecture courses placed freely online. On a similar tack, the Connexions programme at Rice University (Houston, Texas) has explored new models of dynamic peer review scholarship, while simultaneously developing high-quality open educational resources, communally generated by academics. These leading global universities have been making their existing offerings universally available online, providing for a showcase of their teaching practices, a more flexible learning experience for students within and without the university, and a new dimension of institutional morale (Pollak, 2008).

If the amount of free education available to can be increased, will it hurt the economy financially? The job market may increase with the explosion of "educated people" in the field that they are required to have knowledge in. Also, new job opportunities may arise that may not have been available due to previous funding for education. New jobs could be created based on these free online classes. With more skills, employees are better able to perform their duties.

Free educational opportunities could lead the way to employers finding more qualified workers. By providing these courses for free, we could ultimately see our unemployed and underemployed population decrease with an increase in knowledge and quality free education that allows them the potential to find better jobs. We could also see improvement for those who lack motivation due to the high cost of higher education tuition. If people 'choose' to attend school, their motivation increases exponentially. If they are able to attend school for free, they will then be able to spend more time studying and completing courses rather than working several jobs to pay for one credit.

The benefits that free higher education might have on our economy include a much larger population of 16-24 year olds enrolled in college, which in turns leads to more innovative minds joining the workforce. The educational STEM movement in the K-12 public sector of education saw momentum beginning in 2007. It was made clear that in order for our nation to continue to be competitive in our global economy, there needs to be continued education for young adults in the fields of science, technology, engineering, and math. Additionally, if there is a larger shift in this same age group returning to college and completing their degree, it would provide nearly two million jobs to be opened up for the unemployed (Samuels, 2011). Anything that lowers the unemployment rate has a direct impact on the economic state of the nation.

Let's look at public education through the economic viewpoint for our nation. "Currently, only 30% of Americans who start college or university end up graduating, and this represents a huge waste of time and money (Samuels, 2011)." The college student who is attempting to graduate in four years is either faced with an outstanding debt down the road or trying to juggle studies while working at least part-time. This often results in degree completion occurring the fifth or sixth year, while more debt is accrued:

...open access degrees could actually give new

credibility to 'the degree', while simultaneously widening participation in higher learning. Instead of degrees being merely certificates to be bought, worked for, then deployed in the labour market, they would become a more consistent measure of an individual's knowledge and learning capacity, wherever they are from, however old they may be (Pollak, 2008).

As stated by Murray (2012), FLOSS, (free/libre and open source software) is used to help support the lack of education around the world and offset the costs that it takes to receive high quality education. With MOOCs, students are able to take classes designed by educators from high cost schools at little to no cost, depending on their completion diploma. In some cases, paying for an accredited certificate might be required. These ideas are still being worked out with the debate of whether to charge a student to receive an accredited completion certificate or not. Along with MOOCs, Murray (2012) stated that "one of the early FLOSS like developments was the Massachusetts Institute of Technology that piloted in 2002, aiming to put all the educational materials for courses online, freely openly available to anyone, anywhere." This is a huge benefit because too often other parts of lower and middle income countries struggle to have the funds for education. These are the places with the biggest need. In order to address this problem, providing free education with open access models would be a great benefit. What assists with the process of making MOOCs free to all its users is stated by Ruth (2012) "Online classes offer a reduction in labor and administrative costs, therefore decreasing tuition. By providing online classes, many other cost spending areas can be reduced and put more towards teacher pay and online curriculum development."

MOOCs are free for all participants. These students usually earn certificates, but do not earn college credit. However, some MOOCs are incorporating credit towards degrees. It is the goal of education to empower students with more knowledge, therefore leading to more opportunities. Online education through MOOCs can provide many skills for job acquisition and success for the work field. This form of education could be the world's largest equalizer. A way to level out the playing field is to offer free education from highly qualified teachers to anyone around the world who is willing and able to take part in the process.

One of the aims and benefits that MOOCs provides to its users is that the courses are all free. With the increase in the cost of higher education, the reality of fewer people becoming highly educated is apparent. If one cannot afford to go to school, then the choice is no longer there. People are no longer judged on their abilities, but rather measured by their financial situation. If there were more free online classes and degrees, then those who are willing to put in the time and effort toward achieving higher levels of of education would have opportunities they currently do not have.

With the rising cost of college tuition increasing

rapidly over the last thirty years, today's students are reaching the tipping point on whether or not they can afford to attend. How can these potential students afford not attend when every graduating senior is told they need a higher education to gain employment? Yet, after receiving that all-important degree, nearly 54% of graduates were jobless or underemployed in 2011 (Yen, 2012). The offer of a relatively free education might start to sound enticing to the masses. In 2012, Senator Tom Hawkin shared a graph in an email statement, showing that college tuition and fees had indeed increased by 1,120% over the past 35 years (Jamrisko & Kolet, 2012).

In 2011, 85% of college students were enrolled full-time. The United States Bureau of Labor Statistics reported that 53.5% and 50% of these women and men, respectively, were participants in the work force, with another 10.7% of college students listed under the unemployment category (BLS, 2011). Based on those figures, many of today's high school graduates know that they will be working their way through college, unless they are willing to have a large amount of debt as they exit. This will definitely be a determining factor when it comes to school choice, tuition and fees.

It is yet to be seen if MOOCs will drive the cost of tuition down at colleges and universities, or if educational institutions will increase tuition costs further to compensate for those classes students are taking for free. What needs to be recognized as colleges look to lure in students with free MOOCs, is the overall picture of why these classes are so full.

Students can no longer afford the kind of education that is needed for jobs that will offer decent salaries. They end up working too much and ultimately burn out from the struggle to support themselves. When it comes down to the choice of education or work to live, most have to choose the latter.

As the MOOC model currently stands, the monetization of the system may come through the ability to receive certificates for completion of a series of courses covering a skill set or knowledge base being studied. For those recent college graduates who are scraping by in jobs that do not fully use their skills and knowledge, the chance to continue their education, free of charge, may provide that step in the right direction to be noticed by the employers they are seeking. The MOOC start-up company, Coursera, is already providing employers access to student data and scores for a fee (Young, 2012). It remains to be seen whether many companies will invest in this idea and look into hiring prospective employees based solely on proof of skills and certification, yet no degree.

In 2001, two individuals, Bynner and Egerton, published research that showed having a higher education resulted in both men and women being healthier. It is important to keep in mind that the two have somewhat of a causal effect on each other (Bynner & Egerton, 2001). Specifically, if you come from a higher economic background, you are more likely to be healthy and also have more money and influence to attend college than someone from a lower economic standing. The ability that MOOCs provide for anyone to receive a quality education for free can bring about benefits to those looking to create better opportunities and lives for themselves.

· CHAPTER FIVE ·

UNTANGLING FROM THE HYPE

With the climbing costs of tuition there is no wonder that the MOOC has become so popular. The MOOC to many is the answer to growing problems arising with higher education. It is a symbol of change that is greatly needed in order to counteract the growing doubts of the value of higher education. MOOCs offer the possibility to gain a 'world-class education' which was once only available to a select few admitted into Ivy League schools and had the funds to pay for it (Snyder, 2012). MOOCs may have started in the Ivy Leagues, but now the majority of MOOCs are created by other universities and even community colleges. No matter where the knowledge comes from, MOOCs offer this knowledge for free for anyone who has a desire to learn and an internet connection. Although MOOCs provide this knowledge to the masses, this does not guarantee learning. Many debate the effectiveness of online learning and further research is needed to understand what quality of education is gained from an online format.

Formatting the Instruction

The general format of many MOOCs are short video lectures that have quiz questions embedded to check for understanding. Compared to the average college lecture this is not so different. These video lectures are still "one-way, passive instructional models" which only serve to duplicate a practice that is already in existence (Meyer, 2010). An advantage to the scattered quizzes is that students can assess their understanding before moving on, while in a lecture hall this would not be an option. While the format is similar between face-to-face classrooms and some MOOCs, what is missing is the differentiation of instruction that is possible in a face-to-face environment. The U.S. department of Education found that, "elements such as video or online quizzes do not appear to influence the amount that students learn in online classes" (Means et al, 2012). Although students can watch videos at their own pace and even rewind to review something they do not understand, students also have the option to speed up, skim, or even skip videos, which can result in missing important information. While the quizzes are scattered throughout the lecture to monitor student understanding, there is no penalty for an incorrect answer. Students can guess and check and move on without really grasping the important information.

Some believe the internet will do to education what it has done to journalism and print media. Pamela Hieronymi (2012), professor of philosophy at the University of California LA, argues that care should be taken when making this comparison because, "education is not the transmission of information or ideas...but the training needed to make use of information and ideas." In this world of information overload, the skills needed to effectively and efficiently tackle the mounds of information become increasingly important, not less. Computers and the internet are amazing technologies but they do not come close to the insight a teacher can provide by personally knowing students. Watching a series of podcasts and engaging in an online forum discussion with peers is not the same as a teacher intuitively questioning, engaging and challenging a student to grapple with a new concept and then come to a more clear understanding. The sophistication of the online education model simply cannot compare to "one mind engaging with another, in real time: listening, understanding, correcting, modeling, suggesting, prodding, denying, affirming, and critiquing thoughts and their expression" (Hieronymi, 2012). Technology in the form of online learning used as a supplemental tool can improve the quality of education, but if online courses are not designed with extreme care taken to implement research-based best practices, the result could be a lowering of academic standards and a massively open famine of deep understanding.

Learning Guides

It is important not to forget that learning is a process which requires a knowledgeable guide to help organize information, find connections and strengthen understanding in areas to make the whole more complete. Online education takes a route in which people have to work to construct knowledge and understanding. They do not have a guide to lead them, but instead they have to plan, organize, problem-solve, and find tools to help them. Learning online is an independent process that requires "motivation, initiative, and confidence" in order to succeed (Kop, 2011). Although there are those unique individuals who can teach themselves, if a learner does not have these skills they will have a hard time learning in this setting.

Since MOOCs are massive with class sizes reaching into the thousands, learning guides rely heavily on peers. While peer learning has its advantages, as Kirschner (2012) states, "peer learning takes you only so far: at some point, somebody has to know something about the subject". With professors commonly only present in videos, students of MOOCs are often left with little to no guide to help them solve important questions. Dropout rates of MOOCs are often near 90%. A contributing factor to this is that the information progressed too quickly and became far over the average student's head (Thrun, 2012). In a face-to-face classroom, students would have the opportunity to have questions cleared up from the professor, but in a MOOC those questions can be lost or answered incorrectly. Therefore, the first sign of confusion often is not addressed.

The Effectiveness of Peer Graders

With potentially thousands of students in a MOOC class, there is a substantial amount of grading which must be accomplished. There is no question computers are wonderful at grading multiple choice or true false exams. The issue comes when assessments must be completed on students' written essays or short answer tests. One of the ways the MOOC movement is trying to solve this problem is by utilizing peer grading or crowdsource grading. This practice is where each essay or short answer is "graded" by a number of different students and given an average grade. This practice is not new and research has been conducted on the practice with various results. One study, conducted by Philip Sadler, Science Education Department Harvard-Smithsonian Center for Astrophysics, and veteran school teacher Eddie Good (2006), demonstrated that even seventh graders can hold a concept similar to that of the teacher, which is a critical skill to have for peer assessment to work. Their research concluded the peer grades were scored similarly to the grades the teacher gave and recommended responsible use of the practice. They cautioned "if implemented poorly, the grades can be unreliable and students may not learn anything valuable from the process" (Sadler & Good, 2006). Another study conducted by two biology professors at the University of Washington found students were more generous in grading by a factor of 25% over grades determined by their instructors. Despite this, the authors, among many others in the field, support the use of peer-grading because of the role it can play in enhancing student learning (Morrison, 2012). It is hard to argue against the point that students will benefit from being able to review the work of their peers and being able to see how they write and think. Giving the students the opportunity to participate in this type of review process not only saves time for the teacher but helps students recognize their own strengths and weaknesses (Watters, 2012).

However, implementing and monitoring a peer grading system in a class of thirty, as in the Sadler & Good research, is one thing. Doing the same in a class of a thousand or perhaps tens of thousands through the internet is quite another thing. Laura Gibbs, a literature and mythology professor at the University of Oklahoma, gives a telling account of her experience with peer assessment while taking the Fantasy and Science Fiction class through Coursera. In a class of over 5,000 students, she points out that the variability of feedback ranges from "the very zealous" or those with feedback longer than the essay itself to those with a simple "good job" to those who did not take the process serious at all (Watters, 2012). With a class of this size and global reach it is inevitable to find students who have very little experience giving feedback to other students. If the course does not offer support in enhancing this skill, their feedback will suffer along with the learning experience of their fellow students. Another obstacle presents itself by the fact that there are bound to be students in a class of this size and reach whose first language is not English and may not be able to speak English at all. How will these students' peer reviews be considered in the peer assessment system?

Another concern that arises from the implementation of peer grading is the lack of the ability to give feedback on feedback. As a means to protect students' privacy, no one is able to know who has graded one's work nor can one know whom one is grading. One of the benefits of receiving feedback is that you can ask for clarification if needed and commence in a discussion about that feedback. Imagine if a teacher gave you a grade with a load of suggestions/criticisms but you were unable to ask the teacher what was meant by a certain comment or suggestion. It is also nice to know who gives the feedback so one can gauge the value of that feedback based on the author and his/her particular strengths and weaknesses. This anonymity also allows those who wish to disrupt the class by leaving inappropriate and counterproductive comments the shelter to do so because there can be no repercussions (Watters, 2012).

Using peer grading in a small class where students know each other, there is a sense of community with the ability build an environment where feedback is personal and constructive. This is different than trying to do peer grading with thousands of strangers across the face of the globe with varying amounts of skills and subject matter knowledge. One might ask if it is even possible to build a community of peers in this type of environment when participation in forums are not always required and many students visit them seldom if at all. If students are peers only in the fact that they are in the same class and develop very little sense of community and reciprocity, can peer feedback really work? Pamela Hieronymi sums up the issues surrounding this practice stating,

> It is as though elite educators, upon noticing that we can't program a computer to discern what is on the mind of an undergraduate, decided to pretend that if we just let those seeking an education talk among themselves (in grammatically felicitous sentences), they will somehow come to express difficult ideas in persuasive arguments and arrive at coherent, important insights about society, politics, and culture. (2012)

This does not appear to be a valid solution to assessing thousands of students.

Intent and Readiness Levels of MOOC Students

Another important aspect of MOOCs are discussions in which students talk about the week's information. In addition to the video lectures and quizzes, online discussions in which MOOC students can discuss open ended questions is a constructive way for students to process what they have learned and work with other students. Many studies have found that presence, what a person perceives as "real," results in "increased learner satisfaction with online courses and a greater depth of learning" (Pallof & Pratt, 2007, p. 12). With synchronous communication, or chat rooms that are built into a course, students can gain a greater sense of presence since they can share and read ideas with a group in real time. However, these chat rooms can become noisy and random in normal sized classrooms, and with MOOCs these discussions can be nothing less than chaotic. Since MOOCs are so large, supervision of discussions is limited. The openness of MOOCs also makes it "vulnerable to inappropriate behavior" especially since there are no financial risks (Educause, 2011).

Readiness levels of participants of MOOCs also should be taken into consideration. There are many variables for the kind of student entering into a MOOC including their educational background and motivation for joining the class. Since MOOCs are open to the masses without any requirements, a large range of people and readiness levels can participate in the course. While even in the traditional classroom setting there is a range of readiness levels, compared to MOOCs the range is much more narrow since many university courses have prerequisites. Also, since university classes have to be paid for, most students in the class are invested in learning the material.

Pursuing Quality

There are many questions that need to be answered about the quality of education that students gain from MOOCs. Future analysis of MOOCs will need to determine if the MOOC model can offer a world class education to students in courses with class sizes that reach into the hundreds of thousands and if this is comparable to the education gained from traditional classroom settings. There are important questions to consider when courses reach these massive sizes such as if educators are truly effective. Can there truly be a reasonably accurate way to evaluate what a student has gained when there are so many variables? To spread knowledge is one thing, to gain knowledge takes more than a passive act. It is a journey that requires the help of a more knowledgeable guide or guides and a learner who is fully engaged in the process.

· CHAPTER SIX ·

CLIMBING THE LADDER OF ACADEMIC INTEGRITY

One of the advantages of MOOCs is the fact that each class is offered to a profusion of students. This increases the opportunity for the students to sign up for the classes they want. One MOOC could contain more than 160,000 students from all over the world. However, this advantage could be turned into a disadvantage if the students find easy ways to plagiarize, share work, and cheat. Sven Trenholm of Herkimer County Community College (2007), in his review of Cheating in Fully Asynchronous Online Course writes "the idea of academic integrity related to courses taught in a fully online un-proctored modality is therefore of great interest and concern". In this type of course, although they do not offer academic credit, students are finding creative methods to cheat that let them complete the courses with less effort, in ways that are hard to detect because "verifying that the student who has signed up for a MOOC is the same person who has completed the work and taken the exam is, at the moment, a daunting obstacle" (Snyder, 2012). It is certain that MOOC developers are finding a difficult time preventing cheating and plagiarizing. Glenn C. Altschuler, Vice President for University Relations, and David J. Skorton (2013), a president of Cornell University, say "while professors have found ways to promote discussions and collaborative learning among students, we have not yet figured out how to monitor exams to protect against cheating or plagiarism".

Can Massivity Lead to Cheating and Plagiarizing?

The large number of students enrolled in such classes makes it much easier for the students to exchange answers and share their work with their classmates. With this large number of students, the incentive to cheat goes up and the chances of getting caught go down. David Patterson, a professor who runs a MOOC at the University of California, Berkeley says "We found groups of twenty people in a course submitting identical homework" (Webley, 2012). Most of the quizzes and tests in the MOOCs are multiple choice, which makes it a lot easier to share with no evidence of cheating or plagiarizing. In most cases, the students won't be graded by their instructors; instead, software or peer-graded system will be used to do this job. Another reason why cheating is widespread in MOOCs is the ease of creating more than one account because "it might take just five minutes, assuming you spend two devising a stylish user name" (Pappano, 2012). Students can easily create multiple accounts in order to re-take exams. They can take the exam with their fake account to be prepared for the same exam using their actual account.

The Honor Code and Verifying Students' Identity

Websites and software already exist for detecting student work that has evidence of plagiarism. After multiple complaints from Coursera professors about students cheating and plagiarizing assignments Coursera:
> ...instituted an honor code; every time students submit coursework, they have to check a box that says, "In accordance with the Honor Code, I certify that my answers here are my own work, and that I have appropriately acknowledged all external sources (if any) that were used in this work. (Webley, 2012).

MOOC provider Coursera has recently announced a way for students to verify their identity in order to earn a more meaningful certificate or perhaps even college credit one day. An identity verification process, one like Coursera's "Signature Track", is necessary in order to help curb the prolific cheating and plagiarism that has haunted the MOOC movement. Under this "Signature Track" option, students are required to create a profile with a verified picture ID and a photo with their webcam. The software then creates a profile for each students' individual typing pattern by requiring them to type a short phrase. Each time the student logs in to do course work they will have to retype this short phrase to gain access to the course and submit work (Fain, 2013). While this shows some potential, one can easily see where this method could be circumvented without much effort. A student could potentially verify himself, sign into the course and then have someone else sitting by with him to help complete any work.

Taking another approach, MOOC provider edX has decided to offer proctored exams as a way to verify the identity of students and ensure the person taking a test is the person they say they are. They have teamed up with Pearson testing centers to provide this service to students for a minimal fee. Currently, all students who finish a course through edX receive a "certificate of mastery" indicating completion. However, students who opt for the proctored exam will get a certificate indicating such. This certificate still does not earn the student college credit but does serve as a useful tool to authenticate students' work and legitimate the MOOC movement. David Stavens, the chief operating officer at Udacity, claims there is a "compelling case" to be made for the authenticity capabilities of the MOOC movement between in person testing and software that can track a student's participation throughout the term of the course (Kolowich, 2012).

Recently the American Council on Education agreed to review Coursera and several other MOOC courses in order to make a recommendation for whether or not the courses should be granted credit for their completion. The pilot project has many requirements for their test including "authentication of identity," which means that Coursera and other MOOCs have had to make changes to their examinations. These changes include proctored examinations which will prove that students are who they say they are. Coursera has partnered with an online proctoring company "that uses Webcams and software to monitor tests remotely" (Young, 2012). The program requires students to hold up their ID's to their webcam at a specifically scheduled time for the exam and an employee of the company will check to verify their identity. The employee also monitors students as they take their test to see if they are looking on the internet for answers. But there are many problems that arise from this solution. For one, showing ID before an examination does not mean that there isn't someone else in the room to help them answer the questions. Mohamed Noor, a Duke biologist and MOOC instructor, voiced his concerns about the proctored programs saying that the "verification process doesn't show that the work submitted for a class is a solo effort. Any number of people might be sitting with a student while the student types" (Anderson, 2013). While the program is designed to monitor student activity on their computer while taking the test to check for cheating, that does not mean that students cannot look on the internet to find information, many students have smartphones or tablets that they can use which will not show up during the test. While Jarrod Morgan, Vice President of ProctorU, claims each proctor can adequately monitor 4-6 students at once (Michels, 2013), it is hard to imagine this is the case given the various ways students could circumvent the system.

What needs to be remembered is that the MOOC courses being reviewed for the pilot project have much smaller class sizes, and only a handful of courses are being reviewed. There are many things to consider if MOOCs turn toward using proctored examinations in the near future. What will happen when a MOOC is the size of 100,000 people? Nearly 2 million students have registered with Coursera alone, which is a significantly large number to monitor for exams (ACE, 2012). In addition, with the increase of student population, the programs could become less effective and very labor intensive. In a MOOC of 40,000 students, where the average 10% complete all required work and want to take an exam to get the certificate of completion, it would require over 650 proctors (at 6 per student) to monitor the 4000 students taking the exam if it were given at one time. Even spread out throughout a week's time, this is a considerable amount of labor for monitoring that will need to be paid for. This does not seem like a sustainable model of examination monitoring given that the point of a MOOC is to be massive. This method of monitoring looks promising for small class sizes, however, for a massive course like the ones the MOOC movement has been producing, there are too many holes that can be circumvented.

Of course the most glaring obstacle surrounding the proctoring of exams is the potential cost. Currently, each student would pay between $20 and $30 per exam. This does not sound like much money to those of us who spend that amount per week just to get our coffee fix. However, for many students around the world, $30 could be a full month's income. On top of this cost, there are potential additional costs and obstacles that could prevent many students from being able to complete a proctored exam. If a student does not already have a webcam and microphone, the student would be required to purchase one before they could take the exam in order for the proctor to be in constant communication with the student for the duration of the exam. In addition, there is a slew of other technical requirements students must meet before they can gain access to the proctoring system which allows remote access to their computer and screen. Kate Flatley, Student Association vice president of academic affairs-elect at Harpur College, has recently partnered with an online proctoring service for many of its online courses and is strongly opposed to this method of examination claiming, "it's a gross violation of student privacy rights and places an undue financial stress on students as well" (Levina, 2011). Concerns over allowing access to one's computer arise by not knowing if they still have access to the computer after the exam or not knowing what else they can see while the exam is being taken. Will students need to start password protecting all of their files?

Troy University did a pilot program using ProctorU to monitor three sections of its business class where 65 students completed an exam. Although all 65 students did eventually complete the exam and Troy considered the pilot to be a success, there were a number of problems that occurred making it hard to imagine this could be applied to a class population in the thousands. Some of the issues included students missing their scheduled time slot, losing the exam link, missing or non-functioning equipment, inability to reliably authenticate identity, slow bandwidth causing disconnection, and insufficient RAM. Some students ran into a problem when they decided to take the exam on a different computer than the one they used for the class. The software needed to run the exam was not on the new computer. Perhaps most disturbingly of all is the fact that some students took the exam without even using the webcam at all because they could not get it to work. The proctor used only the remote monitoring software to observe the exam for these students, yet their exam was considered a success (Troy University, 2012). How could this be since the main piece of equipment used for monitoring, the webcam, was not even functioning?

If Coursera and other MOOCs are to be considered for accreditation, they will need to make these authenticators mandatory for students. This can mean a significant change for how MOOCs work and are viewed. Since proctored exams have to be done at a specific time or even at specific locations, the convenience of MOOCs can be greatly decreased. Students have to be on the computer or at a testing location at a designated times, which means losing the benefit that MOOCs provide such as being able to work around busy schedules and in the convenience of the home. In addition, the spirit of the MOOC being free and open to everyone will be greatly hindered by adding exam and accreditation fees.

Keeping us Honest

Although MOOCs are free and generally are not available for college credit except in special cases where students have to pay fees, the high amount of cheating and plagiarism that is trending in MOOCs is cause for concern especially when looking into the quality of education the student is getting. While the student may have access to high quality knowledge, if they are to gain that knowledge students have to actively engage and process the information and concepts. David Patterson of UC Berkley described the MOOC environment as "a cheating rich environment" (Wukman, 2012).

Many factors can occur that may drive a student to cheat, some that are out of their control, but although the assignment is complete and turned in, the student has gained, if anything, a surface understanding of the concept. This is due to the little thought that is needed to accomplish the assignment. An important part of many college courses are student essays and MOOCs are no exception to this apart from how they are graded. Many MOOC courses are peer graded, which can be less intimidating for some students since it is not their professor, they may also feel that their peers may not easily notice or take the time to check for plagiarism. Plagiarism is a major problem with MOOCs causing some professors to issue pleas to their thousands of students to stop plagiarizing (Anders, 2012). Since MOOCs have such a large student population and peer grading is needed to provide feedback to the thousands, peer graders in these courses are presented with an "unusual burden" of having to "screen for evidence of cheating in their peers' work" (Anders, 2012). In the cases of plagiarism that have been identified, many include the use of cut-and-paste and patchwork plagiarism.

In addition to plagiarism, another form of cheating is the use of "dummy accounts" that students use in addition to their authentic account. Students use dummy accounts to eventually master multiple choice questions and then take the answers that they know are correct and use them to get perfect or nearly perfect grades (Anders, 2012). This form of cheating does not enhance student learning. Multiple choice questions are in place to check student learning and should be used by students as a tool to measure how close they are to mastering the content and to identify areas that need to be improved.

Although student discussion boards argue

whether or not plagiarism and cheating matter in a free, no credit course, if MOOCs are to be granted more formal credentials this issue will need to be addressed.

· CHAPTER SEVEN ·

IS THE GOLD STAR WORTH IT?

Can MOOCs increase college graduation rates? MOOCs are only just developing, however many colleges and universities are rushing to adopt MOOCs as part of their distance education programs (Lewin, 2013). While MOOCs are beneficial for students who wish to learn with other students from all over the world about a subject of interest, for the most part students do not receive college credit for MOOCs. MOOCs also have poor pass rates, although this could be because there are no requirements for enrollment, and students have no financial commitment (Lewin, 2013). Professor of Statistics at Stanford University Susan Homes states, "I don't think you can get a Stanford education online, just as I don't think that Facebook gives you a social life" (PBS, 2013). Some people who have used social networking sites such as Facebook would agree that social networking doesn't replace human interaction and socializing. Will MOOCs replace face to face education or traditional online education?

Udacity and Coursera College Credit Evaluation

The American Council of Education College Credit Recommendation Service (ACE Credit) will evaluate potential credit for courses offered by Coursera and Udacity (American Council on Education, 2013). Udacity and Coursera are private MOOC providers and offer MOOC courses from several universities (American Council on Education, 2012). Udacity was founded by Sebastian Thrun (former Stanford Professor), David Stavens, and Mike Sokolsky. Coursera was created by Daphne Koller and Andrew Ng (from Stanford University). ACE credit aims to determine if free MOOC online classes provide curriculum similar to traditional college classes. If so, those classes should be eligible for college credit. Coursera has employed teams to assess how much students have learned after completing a Coursera class. Coursera founders believe the ideal outcome would be that students who take the Coursera course for free and who want credit would take a proctored exam where their identification could be verified. If the faculty believes the course should have academic credit, students could pay for a transcript to submit to their chosen college. ACE credit is evaluating pre-algebra, elementary statistics and computer science (American Council on Education, 2012).We should consider if MOOCs will improve degree completion or increase learning.

MOOCs and Credit

Presently, colleges are not required to accept MOOC credits. College credit is currently accepted at over 2,000 schools across the country and for training courses provided by employers or the military. Georgia State University and Colorado State University publically announced their willingness to accept transfer credit for successful completion of specific Moocs (Lewin, 2013).

University of Washington is the first university in the United States to provide MOOC courses for credit. University of Washington is developing MOOC courses in applied mathematics (scientific computing), computer science (with a primary focus on programming), and a sequence in computational finance (University of Washington, 2012). These classes will be free. However, if students wish to take these classes for credit there is an option to enroll in the enhanced instructor led versions for a fee that lead to university credit (Long, 2013). Students in the for credit class would also have direct online communication with the instructor. In free MOOCs students do not have direct communication with instructors. Instead, the top ten most frequently asked questions are addressed directly by the instructor, and the remaining questions may be answered by TA's or peers. In the for credit classes, students also take proctored exams. Students who wish to take classes for credit must also meet the requirements of the educational outreach department. The University of Washington Educational Outreach department aims to select students who will be able to succeed in the MOOC courses. At the time of this writing, there was no information available on University of Washington's website regarding admission requirements for MOOC students.

Pricing for the college credit MOOCs will be similar to the University of Washington credit courses. Pricing on the certificate courses varies, but the courses are typically between $2,000 and $5,000 for a series of three courses (Long, 2013). University of Washington offers several masters degrees and graduate certificate programs online, but University of Washington does not offer any undergraduate degrees online (University of Washington, 2012)

Initially there were very few MOOC courses that offered remedial or introductory courses, which are necessary for lower income students or students who are not ready for college level learning (Altschuler, 2013). Recently, San Jose State University partnered with Udacity to offer MOOC courses. San José State will award credits for select versions of Udacity classes (Young, 2013). The pilot program is available for 300 students from San José community colleges and high schools, and it is hoping to boost student's college readiness. Some of the classes offered will be remedial algebra, college algebra, and statistics and the cost of these classes will be $150, which is 1/10th the tuition of traditional classes (Young, 2013). Even if the classes are low cost, are they really MOOCs? If MOOCs for credit are only available to those who pay a fee, are they really open? If institutions begin charging for MOOC courses they cannot be called MOOCs. Charging fees for MOOCs is not in the spirit of the original MOOC idea.

Remedial and Introductory MOOCs

More than half the students in California's state university system take remedial classes, and these classes cost the students tuition (and financial aid) but they do not count toward graduation requirements. MOOCs might help this problem. The students who are completing MOOCs in their current format are self-motivated learners who already hold more advanced degrees. While many universities are quickly jumping on the MOOC bandwagon, it is not clear how or if MOOCs will work for the beginner or struggling learner. If tuition costs are lowered, will MOOCs expand access to a quality education? Currently, these questions are not directly answered and Thrun admits that MOOCs are "an experiment" (Young, 2013). Even though research is necessary, it should be considered where and on whom this research occurs. At this point, approximately 90 percent of the students who enroll in MOOCs do not complete the class. Even if it is because signing up for the class is easy, a drop-out rate this high will not work for formalized classes. If most universities accept MOOCs for credit this could significantly change or transform the financial aid structure (Laitinen, 2012).

Dozens of additional public universities plan to offer introductory online courses free for credit to anyone in the world in the hope that the students who pass will pay tuition to complete a degree program. The universities including Arizona State University, the University of Cincinnati and the University of Arkansas system will choose which of the existing online courses to convert to an open online course or MOOC in the new program called MOOC2Degree (The Princeton Review, 2013).

Paying for Credit

How can a company offer free online education as an economically sustainable operation? Perhaps one way that a MOOC might become financially sustainable is to offer a MOOC at no charge to the public, but at a cost to those who wish to use it as a substitute for a traditional college course. It is probably inevitable that a MOOC provider will be able to offer a complete university degree for free. It will most likely be financed through prospective employers or online advertising. Will the world of education in the future look like social networking sites?

· CHAPTER EIGHT ·

WRAPPING UP THE MOOCS

MOOCs show promise and also present challenges. They can bring college level online courses, including courses from Ivy League schools, to anyone with an internet connection anywhere in the world at no cost. MOOCs can help people advance professionally and expand their personal and academic networks. They demonstrate innovation in education, interactive learning, active learning environments through online education, and free online education for a diverse student population from around the world. The challenges MOOCs face surround the issues of large class size, varying college readiness levels, academic integrity, and whether MOOC courses will be universally accepted for college credit.

Are MOOCs the answer to the state of college

education today? As they continue to improve, MOOCs may be the disruptive innovation that will change higher education as we know it. The surge in popularity of MOOCs occurred at the point where college tuition had increased by more than 600 percent in the prior 30 years, while wages had remained stagnant. Tamar Lewin, education writer for the New York Times writes, "Lower-tier colleges, already facing resistance over high tuition, may have trouble convincing students that their courses are worth the price," (Lewin, 2012).

While online education can be an effective form of learning, there is no guarantee students will learn from MOOCs. It is easier to procrastinate in online courses. Some students may only check in once a week to view lectures, submit assignments and participate in online discussions. For students to learn the material, they need to be actively engaged in the processes. Many MOOCs have implemented new technologies that require student engagement. It is important that course providers, designers and teachers find ways to engage students and motivate them to complete the courses.

When students are taking a class in a physical classroom today, the teaching method is designed for the whole class instead of individual needs in terms of pace, content delivery method, activities, and assessment practices. MOOCs allow individual learning needs to be met through automated process and avenues such as student interaction. Students can interact with one another through a variety of ways such as social networks or Google hangouts where students can interact with one another through voice or through a web cam. This simulates a face to face situation online. Students can also participate with one another through course discussion threads, and in many MOOCs discussion thread participation is part of the grade. In many MOOCs, the instructor plays the supporting role and the learning happens through student interaction.

Online education allows students to participate in active learning environments where students work together to learn new material. Students can learn new concepts in a variety of forms such as discussions, interactive videos, interactive multimedia activities, and readings. There are over 2.5 million students enrolled in MOOCs, and students from all over the world are sharing their knowledge with everyone. MOOC learning environments allow students to have broad access to diverse interaction because of its unlimited course size. This allows students to process information in ways that would not be available in smaller classes.

Nearly all MOOCs today are free, and while free MOOCs do not usually directly lead to college credit, MOOCs do offer many benefits. Since so many students are taking these courses, this may be a way to reduce educational costs and increase access to education. MOOCs could help increase educational attainment worldwide. Free education could lead to a consistent measure of knowledge instead of a degree that is purchased. MOOCs allow students to enroll in Ivy League classes, and therefore there is fear that they may eliminate low-tier universities. MIT professor Walter Lewis predicts, "that a fair fraction of the very bad universities in the US will disappear. It may take 10 years, it may take 20 years, but that is going to happen" (Parr, 2013). In the future students may be able to take classes, and perhaps even complete degrees, through MOOC providers instead of enrolling at a less prestigious college.

While MOOCs have many benefits, there are drawbacks including large class sizes, varying college readiness levels, discussion quality, high attrition, and lack of teacher feedback. Successful learning in an online class requires that students have motivation, initiative, and confidence. When students lack these qualities they will have a difficult time learning in an online environment. University of British Columbia Professor and education writer from RR Teaching, Rosie Redfield likens MOOC attrition rate with exercise bikes. She explains that the student:

> . . . somehow loses motivation. Just like with that exercise bike, they feel bad about dropping out, and really wish they could have continued. Sometimes they will have stopped for a solid reason (bike equivalent - sprained ankle), but for many it was just lack of motivation. They know that they're missing a lot by not keeping up with the work, but their motivation fades and they're left with another failed attempt at learning. (Redfield, 2012)

Since MOOCs are available to anyone with an internet connection, another reason for the high drop-out rate might be college readiness. However, MOOCs may be the solution to this problem because there are an increasing number of remedial MOOCs offered. Students can receive the remedial help they need at no cost instead of paying for similar courses in traditional colleges. Since remedial courses in colleges do not count for college credit, this may be an attractive alternative.

Even though the majority of MOOCs are free and do not offer college credit, the high incidence of cheating and plagiarism is concerning. Students who take classes through some providers will be able to take a proctored exam in person at an international network of testing centers. EdX's first president Professor Anant Agarwal says, "This is a very important step because people have been concerned that learners had no way of showing that they had done the work themselves, if they were applying for a job or for higher education" (Coughlan, 2012). If MOOCs for credit become ubiquitous, issues regarding cheating, plagiarism and identity verification will need to be addressed.

MOOC courses are not universally accepted for credit, but many colleges are offering MOOC courses for credit. However, most charge a fee, so they aren't really free or open for credit, and therefore not technically MOOCs. The American Council on Education recommended 5 MOOC courses for credit offered through Coursera. Steve Kolowish, journalist from The Chronicle of Higher Education reports that even though Duke University, University of California at Irvine, and University of Pennsylvania are offering MOOC courses for credit, it is still up to the degree granting institution to decided if the college will accept MOOC credits (Kolowich, 20013).

It is unlikely that MOOCs will radically change every college class. They also are not the easy solution to education's financial crisis (University of Washington MOOCs cost the same as University of Washington online classes). MOOCs are a tool that can be used to deliver courses online. If MOOCs are to become the disruptive innovation many people fear or hope for, they will have to resist efforts to turn this innovation into a sustaining innovation serving only to support the existing systems. If MOOCs are offered for college credit, a higher degree of acceptance and respect will be achieved. However, if students have to pay for that college credit, the dream of free and open education will have been hijacked. The innovation will be truly disruptive only if the college credit problem is solved, either by providing a system whereby students can earn college credit at no cost, or by sidestepping the issue entirely through development of an alternative schema of recognition of mastery of learning.

Chris Fiend, contributor to Hybrid Pedagogy (A Digital Journal of Teaching and Technology), writes, "The promise of MOOCs lies not in what the format lets us do, but in what the format lets us question: Where does learning happen? What are the requirements of effective collaboration? How can assessment become more authentic? How much structure and direction are best in a classroom" (Fiend, 2012)? These are all important questions to consider as MOOCs continue to transform the educational landscape in the digital age.

What is the future of MOOCs? Will MOOCs be used as a tool in higher learning or will they completely dismantle our higher education system? Kevin Carey, director of the education-policy program at the New American Foundation describes the college monopoly on the sale of college credits as very valuable things to control. Carey predicts that MOOCs will "accelerate the breakup of the college credit monopoly" (Carey, 2012). Whether one welcomes or fears such an outcome, it is clear that there are powerful interests at play, and there will be those in the traditional educational system who must either neutralize the threat - by turning the technologies and innovations behind MOOCs into sustaining innovations - or risk losing their livelihoods.

Henry David Thoreau wrote, "We boast of our system of education, but why stop at schoolmasters and schoolhouses? We are all schoolmasters, and our schoolhouse is the universe" (Thoreau, 1859). The idea that every student should strive to attend a brick and mortar school may be a relic of the past. Our schoolhouse may become the internet and the schoolhouse is available to everyone, regardless of location or life circumstances. MOOCs are causing educators and administrators to reexamine our current understanding of learning and how online education is changing and reinventing itself.

MOOCs may be here to stay and may revolutionize education. They may turn out to be an interesting flash in the pan of history. They may be transformed into just another way to attend university classes, where students will have to pay tuition. Whatever happens, MOOCs have irrevocably changed the world of education in that they have proven several crucial points. First, they have proven that it is possible to provide free education in the form of free online classes. Second, they have proven that there is both interest and demand for free education. Finally, they have proven dramatically that the quality of education available at the world's most expensive institutions can also be available to the masses at no cost. Although much of the discussion in these pages has been about the potential in this movement, massive open online courses have already changed the world. Now it is imperative that we understand these changes and help guide our future toward maximum benefit for all.

Anyone with an interest in education would do well to continue following the developments in this exciting area. It may turn out to be the innovation that allows education to become universally available to everyone regardless of location or financial situation. And if it does, it will completely revolutionize what it means to be an educator and what it means to be a student.

· BIBLIOGRAPHY ·

Abajian, S., Dewaard, I., Gallagher, M., Hogue, R., Keskin, N., Koutropoulos, A., and Rodriguez, O. (2011). Using Mlearning and MOOCs to Understand Chaos, Emergence, and Complexity in Education. The international View of Research in Open and Distance Learning, 12 (7).

Abernathy, J. (2013, January 25). To MOOC Or Not to MOOC [Web Log Comment]. Retrieved from http://www.insidehighered.com/blogs/alma-mater/mooc-or-not-mooc

American Council On Education. (2012). Ace to Assess Potential of MOOCs, Evaluate Courses for Credit-Worthiness. Retrieved from: http://www.acenet.edu/news-room/pages/ace-to-assess-potential-of-moocs,-evaluate-courses-for-credit-worthiness.aspx

Anders, George. (2012). Are They Learning Or Cheating? Online Teaching's Dilemmas. forbes. Retrieved from: http://www.forbes.com/sites/georgeanders/2012/0

BIBLIOGRAPHY

8/16/are-they-learning-or-cheating-online-teachings-dilemma/

Anderson, Nick. (2013). MOOCs- Here Come The Credentials. The Washington Post. Retrieved from http://www.washingtonpost.com/blogs/college-inc/post/moocs--here-come-the-credentials/2013/01/09/a1db85a2-5a67-11e2-88d0-c4cf65c3ad15_blog.html

Arum, R., Roksa, J., & Cho, E. (2011). Improving Undergraduate Learning: Findings and Policy Recommendations from the Ssrc-Cla Longitudinal Project. Retrieved from http://highered.ssrc.org/wp-content/uploads/2012/01/improving-undergraduate-learning-2011.pdf

Associated Press (2012, April 23). Half of Recent College Grads Underemployed or Jobless, Analysis Says. Retrieved from http://www.cleveland.com/business/index.ssf/2012/04/half_of_recent_college_grads_u.html

Associated Press (2012, October 23). Number of active users at Facebook over the years. Retrieved from http://finance.yahoo.com/news/number-active-users-facebook-over-years-214600186--finance.html

Associated Press. (1989, August 28). Most Teachers Think Computers are Boon to Schools, Poll Says. The Deseret News. Retrieved from http://news.google.com/newspapers?id=cawpaaaaibaj&sjid=tiqdaaaaibaj&pg=6776,5260983

Bianchi, W. (2008). Education by Radio: America's Schools of The Air. Techtrends, 52(2), 36-44.

Blackmon, S. J. (2012). Outcomes of Chat and Discussion Board Use in Online Learning: A Research Synthesis. Journal of Educators Online, 9(2)

Bls. United States Department of Labor, Bureau of Labor Statistics. (2011). College Enrollment and Work Activity of 2011 High School Graduates. Retrieved from Website:

http://www.bls.gov/news.release/hsgec.nr0.htm

Boxall, M. (2012, August 08). MOOCs: A Massive Opportunity for Higher Education, Or Digital Hype? [Web Log Comment]. Retrieved from http://www.guardian.co.uk/higher-education-network/blog/2012/aug/08/mooc-coursera-higher-education-investment

Bradley, P. (2012). Invasion of the MOOCs. Community College Week, 25(9), 6.

Brooks, David. (2012). The Campus Tsunami. The New York Times. Retrieved from http://www.nytimes.com/2012/05/04/opinion/brooks-the-campus-tsunami.html

Bustillos, M. (2013, January 31). Venture Capital's Massive, Terrible Idea for The Future of College. Retrieved from http://www.theawl.com/2013/01/venture-capitals-massive-terrible-idea-for-the-future-of-college

Bynner, J., & Egerton, M. (2001). The Wider Benefits of Higher Education. Retrieved from http://dera.ioe.ac.uk/5993/3/01_46_part3.pdf

Carey, K. (2012). Into The Future With MOOCs. Chronicle of Higher Education, 59(2), 29.

Carr, N. (2012, September 27). The Crisis in Higher Education. Retrieved from http://www.technologyreview.com/featuredstory/429376/the-crisis-in-higher-education/

Christensen, C. (2011). Disrupting Class. New York: Mcgraw-Hill.

Cleveland-Innes, M., & Ally, M. (2012). Learning to Feel: Education, Affective Outcomes and the Use of Online Teaching and Learning. Learning. Retrieved from http://www.eurodl.org/?article=285

Cohn, S. (2012, October 18). Student Loan Debt Hits Record High, Study Shows. Retrieved from http://www.nbcnews.com/business/student-loan-debt-hits-record-high-study-shows-1c6542975

BIBLIOGRAPHY

Corbyn, Z. (2012, 12 6). This Could Be Huge. Time Higher Education. Retrieved from http://www.timeshighereducation.co.uk/story.asp?storycode=422034

Cost, J., Miller, J., Mcleod, J., George, M., Haro, P., & Mahler, J. (2013, January 14). Unthinking Technophilia. Retrieved from http://www.insidehighered.com/views/2013/01/14/essay-says-faculty-involved-moocs-may-be-making-rope-professional-hangings

Coughlan, S. (2012, October 31). How Do You Stop Online Students Cheating? Retrieved February 10, 2013, From Bbc News Business: http://www.bbc.co.uk/news/business-19661899

Coursera. (2013, March 29). Website. Retrieved from https://www.coursera.org/

Crotty, J. (2012). Distance Learning Has Been Around Since 1892, You Big MOOC. Forbes. Retrieved from http://www.forbes.com/sites/jamesmarshallcrotty/2012/11/14/distance-learning-has-been-around-since-1892-you-big-mooc/

Curran, T. (2013, February 19). MOOCs Can Save Students, Not Just Dollars. [Web Log Comment] Retrieved from http://www.tedcurran.net/2013/02/moocs-can-save-students-not-just-dollars/

Dae Shik, K., Lee, H., & Skellenger, A. (2012). Comparison of Levels of Satisfaction With Distance Education and On-Campus Programs. Journal of Visual Impairment & Blindness, 106(5), 275-286

Disalvio, P. (2012, November 20). Bubble Wrap: Higher Education and The Value Gap. Retrieved from http://www.nebhe.org/thejournal/bubble-wrap-higher-education-and-the-value-gap/

Educause. (2011). 7 Things You Should Know About MOOCs. Educause: Learning initiative. Retrieved from:

http://net.educause.edu/ir/library/pdf/eli7078.pdf

Educause. (2012). 2012 Students and Technology. Retrieved from http://net.educause.edu/ir/library/pdf/ers1208/eig1208.pdf

Ellis, Z. (N.D.). 5 Basic Ways MOOCs Can Be Valuable to Traditional Students. Retrieved from http://www.teachthought.com/learning/5-basic-ways-moocs-can-be-valuable-to-traditional-students/

Elvers, G. C., Polzella, D. J., & Graetz, K. (2003). Procrastination in Online Courses: Performance and attitudinal Differences. Teaching of Psychology, 30(2), 159-162.

Fain, P. (2013, January 9). Paying for Proof. Retrieved from http://www.insidehighered.com/news/2013/01/09/courseras-fee-based-course-option#.uo2as-j-rn4.email

Federal Reserve Bank of New York, Research and Statistics Group. (2013). Household Debt and Credit Report. Retrieved from Website: http://www.newyorkfed.org/householdcredit/

Fiend, C. (2012, August 24). Learning As Performance: MOOC Pedagogy and On-Ground Classes. Retrieved February 2012, 7, From Hybrid Pedagogy A Digital Journal of Teaching and Technology: http://www.hybridpedagogy.com/journal/files/mooc_pedagogy.html

Flicker, Allison. (2013). Massive Open Online Classes Raises Questions About The Future of Education. NBC News. Retrieved from: http://dailynightly.nbcnews.com/_news/2013/01/31/16795195-massive-open-online-classes-raise-questions-about-future-of-education?lite

Friedman, Thomas L. (2013). Revolution Hits The Universities. The New York Times. Retrieved from: http://www.nytimes.com/2013/01/27/opinion/sun

BIBLIOGRAPHY

day/friedman-revolution-hits-the-universities.html?hp

Graham G. (2012). How The Embrace of MOOCs Could Hurt Middle America. Chronicle of Higher Education, 59(6), B22-B23.

Harden, N. (2013, Jan/Feb). The End of the University As We Know It. The American interest. Retrieved from http://the-american-interest.com/article.cfm?piece=1352

Heeyoung, H., & Johnson, S. D. (2012). Relationship Between Students' Emotional intelligence, Social Bond, and interactions in Online Learning. Journal of Educational Technology & Society, 15(1), 78-89.

Hieronymi, P. (2012, August 13). Don't Confuse Technology With College Teaching. Retrieved from http://chronicle.com/article/dont-confuse-technology-with/133551/

Horowitz, E. (2013, February 6). Why Should We Preserve The Higher Education System? [Web Log Comment] Retrieved from http://www.peerreviewedbymyneurons.com/2013/02/06/why-should-we-preserve-the-higher-education-system/

Howard, J. (2012). Can MOOCs Help Sell Textbooks?. Chronicle of Higher Education, 59(4), 19.

Hunt, G. (2011). Disruptive Technology Is Driving New Ways of Learning. Retrieved from http://www.tclabz.com/2011/07/24/disruptive-technology-is-driving-a-new-way-of-learning/

Jakobsdóttir, S., Mckeown, L., & Hoven, D. (2010). Using The New information and Communication Technologies for The Continuing Professional Development of Teachers Through Open and Distance Learning. Learning.

Jamrisko, M., & Kolet, I. (2012, August 15). Cost of College Degree in U.S. Soars 12 Fold: Chart of The Day. Retrieved from http://www.bloomberg.com/news/2012-08-15/cost-of-college-degree-in-u-s-soars-12-fold-chart-of-the-day.html

Kaya, T. (2010, 09 16). [Web Log Message]. Retrieved from http://chronicle.com/blogs/wiredcampus/enrollment-in-online-courses-increases-at-the-highest-rate-ever/28204

Kirschner, A. (2012). A Pioneer in Online Education Tries A MOOC. Chronicle of Higher Education, 59(6), B21.

Klapp , A. (2013). MOOCs Open Doors for Diverse Student Body. Diversity Journal, Feb 5, 2013.

Kolowich, S. (2012, September 07). MOOCing On Site. Retrieved from http://www.insidehighered.com/news/2012/09/07/site-based-testing-deals-strengthen-case-granting-credit-mooc-students

Kolowich, S. (2013). American Council On Education Recommends 4 MOOCs for Credit. Retrieved February 10, 2013, From The Chronicle of Higher Education: http://chronicle.com/article/american-council-on-education/137155/

Kolowich, S. (2013). Universities Try MOOCs in Bid to Lure Successful Students to Online Programs. The Chronicle of Higher Education. Retrieved from https://chronicle.com/blogs/wiredcampus/universities-try-mooc2degree-courses-to-lure-successful-students-to-online-programs/41829

Kop, R. and Hill, A. (2008). Connectivism: Learning Theory of The Future Or Vestige of The Past? International Review of Research in Open and Distance Learning, 9 (3).

Laitinen, A. (2012, July 17). Is This The Beginning of A Sea Change in Higher Ed. Retrieved Jan 29, 2013, From Higher Ed Watch: http://higheredwatch.newamerica.net/blogposts/201

BIBLIOGRAPHY

2/is_this_the_beginning_of_a_sea_change_in_higher_ed-69635

Larreamendy-Joerns, J. and Leinhardt, G. (2006). Going The Distance With Online Education. American Educational Research Association, 76 (4), 567-605.

Lenoue, M., Hall, T., & Eighmy, M. A. (2011). Adult Education and the Social Media Revolution. Adult Learning, 22(2), 4-12.

Levina, Y. (2011, May 10). Webcam Proctors Raise Questions of Privacy. Retrieved from http://www.bupipedream.com/news/6178/webcam-proctors-raise-questions-of-privacy/

Lewin, T. (2012, November 19). College of Future Could Be Come One, Come All. Retrieved February 10, 2013, From New York Times: http://www.nytimes.com/2012/11/20/education/colleges-turn-to-crowd-sourcing-courses.html?pagewanted=all&_r=0

Lewin, T. (2013, January 23). Public Universities to offer Free Online Classes for Credit. New York Times. Retrieved February 1, 2013, From http://www.nytimes.com/2013/01/23/education/public-universities-to-offer-free-online-classes-for-credit.html?partner=rss&emc=rss&_r=0

Lewin, T. (2012). College Credit Eyed for Online Courses. New York Times. Retrieved from http://www.nytimes.com/2012/11/14/education/moocs-to-be-evaluated-for-possible-college-credit.html?_r=0

Lionarakis, A. (2012). The Theory of Distance Education and Its Complexity. Learning.

Liu, X., Magjuka, R. J., Bonk, C. J., & Lee, S. (2007). Does Sense of Community Matter? An Examination of Participants' Perceptions of Building Learning Communities in Online Courses. Quarterly Review of Distance Education, 8(1), 9-88.

Long, K. (2013, July 18). Uw to offer Fee-Based Courses

Through Coursera. Retrieved February 1, 2013, From The Seattle Times: http://seattletimes.com/html/localnews/2018714077_coursera19m.html

Ltschuler, D. K. (2013, January 28). MOOCs: A College Education Online? Retrieved February 2013, 1, From forbes: http://www.forbes.com/sites/collegeprose/2013/01/28/moocs-a-college-education-online/

Mangan, K. (2012). MOOC Mania. Chronicle of Higher Education, 59(6), B4-B5.

Maslow, A. (1970). Motivation and Personality. (P. 92). New York: Harper & Row.

Masters, K. (2013). A Brief Guide to Understanding MOOCs. The internet Journal of Medical Education. 2011 Volume 1 Number 2.

McLeod, S. A. (2007). Vygotsky. Simply Psychology. Retrieved from http://www.simplypsychology.org/vygotsky.html

Mcneely, I., & Wolverton, L. (2008). Reinventing Knowledge, From Alexandria to the internet. New York: Norton & Company.

Means, B., Toyama, Y., Murphy, R., Bakia, M., & Jones, K. U.S. Department of Education, (2010). Evaluation of Evidence-Based Practices in Online Learning: A Meta-Analysis and Review of Online Learning Studies. Retrieved from http://www2.ed.gov/rschstat/eval/tech/evidence-based-practices/finalreport.pdf

Meyer, K. (2010, March 3). The Role of Disruptive Technology in the Future of Higher Education. Retrieved from http://www.educause.edu/ero/article/role-disruptive-technology-future-higher-education

Michels, S. (2013, January 08). Catching Cheaters On Open Online Courses. Retrieved from

BIBLIOGRAPHY

http://www.pbs.org/newshour/rundown/2013/01/how-to-make-sure-online-students-dont-cheat.html

Morrison, D. (2012, July 6). Peer Grading in Online Classes: Does It Work? Retrieved from http://onlinelearninginsights.wordpress.com/2012/07/06/peer-grading-in-online-classes-does-it-work/

Murray, P. (2012). Will 'Free' and 'Open' rule The Day As The Future of Online Education. Online Journal of Nursing informatics (Ojni), 16(3).

N.A. (2013) "MOOC 2.0" offers Free, for-Credit Education On Demand; World Education University Is The First and Only Free, Degree-Granting, Online College. World Education University, Heraldonline.Com. Retrieved from http://www.prnewswire.com/news-releases/mooc-20-offers-free-for-credit-education-on-demand-world-education-university-is-the-first-and-only-free-degree-granting-online-college-189793781.html

NCES. (2011). The Condition of Education. Retrieved from http://nces.ed.gov/programs/coe/tables/table-cst-1.asp

NCES. (2011). Total Fall Enrollment in Degree-Granting institutions, by attendance Status, Sex of Student, and Control of institution: Selected Years, 1947 Through 2010. Retrieved from http://nces.ed.gov/programs/digest/d11/tables/dt11_198.asp?referrer=report

NMC. & Educause, (2013). NMC Horizon Project Preview 2013 Higher Education Edition. NMC Horizon Project. Retrieved from http://www.nmc.org/pdf/2013-horizon-higher-ed-preview.pdf

National Council for Curriculum and Assessment. (n.d.). Learning and developing through interaction. Retrieved from http://www.ncca.ie/en/Curriculum_and_Assessmen

t/Early_Childhood_and_Primary_Education/Early_Childhood_Education/Aistear_Toolkit/interactions.pdf

Noonoo, S. (2013, January 16). How Disruptive Technologies Are Leading The Next Great Education Revolution. Retrieved from http://thejournal.com/articles/2013/01/14/how-disruptive-technologies-are-leading-the-next-great-education-revolution.aspx

Palloff, R., Pratt, K. (2010). Building Online Learning Communities: Effective Strategies for The Virtual Classroom. Jossey-Bass. San Francisco, Ca.

Pappano, L. (2012). The Year of The MOOC. New York Times. Retrieved from http://www.nytimes.com/2012/11/04/education/edlife/massive-open-online-courses-are-multiplying-at-a-rapid-pace.html?pagewanted=all&_r=4&

Parr, C. (2013, February 7). Two Decades to Take Out The 'Trash', MOOC-Style. Retrieved February 10, 2013, From Times Higher Education: http://www.timeshighereducation.co.uk/story.asp?sectioncode=26&storycode=422586&c=1

PBS. (2013, January 8). How Free Online Courses Are Changing The Traditional Liberal Arts Education. Retrieved January 21, 2013, From PBS News Hour: http://www.pbs.org/newshour/bb/education/jan-june13/online_01-08.html

Pew Research. (2011, May 15). Is College Worth It?. Retrieved from http://www.pewsocialtrends.org/2011/05/15/is-college-worth-it/4/

Pollak, L. (2008). Should Higher Education Course Materials Be Free to All?. Public Policy Research, 15(1), 36-41.

Popenici, S., and Kerr, S. (2013). What Undermines Higher Education. Popenici: Lexington, KY.

Popkin, H. (2012, December 4). We spent 230,060 years

on social media in one month. Retrieved from http://www.cnbc.com/id/100275798/We_Spent_230060_Years_on_Social_Media_in_One_Month

Redfield, D. R. (2012, October 9). Avoiding the 'Exercise Bike' Problem With MOOCs. Retrieved February 10, 2013, From Rrteaching: http://rrteaching.blogspot.com/2012/10/avoiding-exercise-bike-problem-with.html

Rees, R. (2013, January 10). The Manager's Brain Under The Workman's Cap. [Web Log Comment]. Retrieved from http://moreorlessbunk.wordpress.com/2013/01/10/the-managers-brain-under-the-workmans-cap/

Rees, R. (2013, January 14). So I Signed Up for Another MOOC. [Web Log Comment]. Retrieved from http://moreorlessbunk.wordpress.com/2013/01/14/so-i-signed-up-for-another-mooc/

Reich, J. (2012, May 7). Summarizing All MOOCs in One Slide: Market, Open and Dewey. Ed Tech Researcher [Web Log Comment]. Retrieved from http://blogs.edweek.org/edweek/edtechresearcher/2012/05/all_moocs_explained_market_open_and_dewey.html

Robison, J. (2013, January 16). A New Role for Faculty in The Virtual Classroom. Retrieved from http://www.evolllution.com/distance_online_learning/a-new-role-for-faculty-in-the-virtual-classroom/?utm_source=rss&utm_medium=rss&utm_campaign=a-new-role-for-faculty-in-the-virtual-classroom%20

Rodriguez, C. O. (2012). MOOCs and The AI-Stanford Like Courses: Two Successful and Distinct Course formats for Massive Open Online Courses. Learning. Retrieved from http://www.eurodl.org/index.php?article=516

Royer, S. (2012, November 29). Interview by C Horton [Video Tape Recording]. Your Business Should

Embrace MOOCs. Marketing Technology Minute. Retrieved from http://www.youtube.com/watch?&v=bycqwu9-ao4

Rushkoff, Douglas. (2013). Online Courses Need Human Element to Educate. Cnn. Retrieved from http://www.cnn.com/2013/01/15/opinion/rushkoff-moocs/index.html

Ruth, S. (2012). Can MOOCs and Existing E-Learning Efficiency Paradigms Help Reduce College Costs?. Available at Ssrn 2086689.

Sadler, P., & Good, E. (2006). The Impact of Self- and Peer-Grading On Student Learning. Education Assessment,11(1), 1-31.

Samuels, B. (2011, November 18). Why All Public Higher Education Should Be Free. Huffington Post College. Retrieved from http://www.huffingtonpost.com/bob-samuels/why-all-public-higher-edu_b_1099437.html

Samuels, B. (2013, January 9). A Failure of interaction: A Report From The Ucla forum On High-Tech Higher Education. [Web Log Comment]. Retrieved from http://changinguniversities.blogspot.com/2013/01/a-failure-of-interaction-report-from.html

Schejbal, D. (2013, January 25). Politics, Money and Public Higher Education: A Perfect Storm. Retrieved from http://www.evolllution.com/featured/politics-money-and-public-higher-education-a-perfect-storm/?utm_source=rss&utm_medium=rss&utm_campaign=politics-money-and-public-higher-education-a-perfect-storm

Schlegel, A., Rudelson, J., & Tse, P. (2012). White Matter Structure Changes As Adults Learn A Second Language. Journal of Cognitive Neuroscience, 24(8), 1664-1670.

Sheehy, K. (2013, 01 08). [Web Log Message]. Retrieved from http://www.usnews.com/education/online-education/articles/2013/01/08/online-course-

BIBLIOGRAPHY

enrollment-climbs-for-10th-straight-year

Simon, G. (2013). Are Massive Open Online Courses (MOOCs) Changing Education? Technorati. Retrieved from http://technorati.com/technology/article/are-massive-open-online-courses-moocs/

Skorton, Altschuler, D. (2013, January 28). MOOCs: A College Education Online?. forbes, Retrieved from http://www.forbes.com/sites/collegeprose/2013/01/28/moocs-a-college-education-online/

Snyder, M. D. (2012). Much Ado About MOOCs. Academe, 98(6), 55.

Snyder, M. M. (2009). instructional-Design Theory to Guide The Creation of Online Learning Communities for Adults. Techtrends: Linking Research and Practice to Improve Learning, 53(1), 48-56.

Social Constructivism. (N.D.). Teaching Guide for Gsis. University of California Berkley, N.D. Retrieved from:
http://gsi.berkeley.edu/teachingguide/theories/social.html

Stommel, J., Morris, S.M. (2012, November 19). A MOOC Is Not A Thing: Emergence, Disruption, and Higher Education. [Web Log Comment]. Retrieved from http://www.hybridpedagogy.com/journal/files/mooc_emergence_disruption_and_higher_education.html

Strijbos, J. W. (2000). A Classification Model for Group-Based Learning. Retrieved from http://www.eurodl.org/?p=archives&year=2000&article=86

The Princeton Review. (2013, January 25). The Latest On The MOOC Scene: A New Opportunity for Transfer of Credit An incentive to Enroll and A "Bill of Rights" for Online Students. Retrieved February 2013, 1, From The Princeton Review: http://in.princetonreview.com/in/2013/01/the-latest-on-the-mooc-scene-a-new-opportunity-for-transfer-credit-an-incentive-to-enroll-and-a-bill.html

Thoreau, H. D. (1859, October 15). Library - The Henry D. Thoreau Quotation Page: Conservation. Retrieved February 7, 2013, From The Walden Woods Project: http://www.walden.org/library/quotations/conservation

Toyama, K. (2011, January). There Are No Technology Shortcuts to Good Education. Retrieved from https://edutechdebate.org/ict-in-schools/there-are-no-technology-shortcuts-to-good-education/

Trenholm, S. (2007). A Review of Cheating in Fully Asynchronous Online Courses: A Math Or Fact-Based Course Perspective. Journal of Educational Technology Systems, 35(3), 281-300.

Troy University. (2012, June 26). About Proctoru. Retrieved from http://business.troy.edu/portal/about-proctoru.aspx

Tschofen, C., & Mackness, J. (2012). Connectivism and Dimensions of individual Experience. International Review of Research in Open & Distance Learning, 13(1), 124-143.

University of Washington. (2012, July 18). University of Washington Is The First in U.S. to Provide Credit Classes and Certificate Programs On MOOC Platform. Retrieved February 1, 2013, From Professional and Continuing Education: http://www.pce.uw.edu/newsroom.aspx?id=10865

Vollmer, T. (2012) Keeping MOOCs Open. Creative Commons. [Web log comment] Retrieved from https://creativecommons.org/weblog/entry/34852

Walker, J., (2013). Why MOOCs Might Be Hindered By The Definition of Correspondence Education. Retrieved from http://dx.doi.org/10.2139/ssrn.2208066

Watters, A. (2012, August 27). The Problems With Peer Grading in Coursera. Retrieved from

BIBLIOGRAPHY

http://www.insidehighered.com/blogs/hack-higher-education/problems-peer-grading-coursera

Webley, K. (2012, November 19). MOOC Brigade: Can Online Courses Keep Students From Cheating?. Retrieved from http://nation.time.com/2012/11/19/mooc-brigade-can-online-courses-keep-students-from-cheating/

Weissmann, J. (2012, April 23). 53% of Recent College Grads Are Jobless Or Underemployed—How? The atlantic. Retrieved from http://www.theatlantic.com/business/archive/2012/04/53-of-recent-college-grads-are-jobless-or-underemployed-how/256237/

Weissmann, J. (2012, July 3). Why the internet Isn't Going to End College As We Know It. The atlantic. Retrieved from http://www.theatlantic.com/business/archive/2012/07/why-the-internet-isnt-going-to-end-college-as-we-know-it/259378/

Wukman, Alex. (2012). Coursera Battered With Accusations of Plagiarism and High Drop-Out Rates. Online College. Retrieved from http://www.onlinecolleges.net/2012/08/22/coursera-battered-with-accusations-of-plagiarism-and-high-drop-out-rates/

Yen, H. (2012, April 23). 1 in 2 New Graduates Are Jobless Or Underemployed. Yahoo News. Retrieved from http://news.yahoo.com/1-2-graduates-jobless-underemployed-140300522.html

Yirka, B. (2011, April 5). Research Shows Adult Brains Capable of Rapid New Growth. Retrieved from http://phys.org/news/2011-04-adult-brains-capable-rapid-growth.html

Young , S. & Bruce, M. (2011). Classroom Community and Student Engagement in Online Courses. Journal of Online Learning and Teaching. Retrieved from http://jolt.merlot.org/vol7no2/young_0611.htm

Young, J. (2012). MOOCs Take A Major Step toward Qualifying for College Credit. Chronicle of Higher Education, 59(13), A23.

Young, J. (2012, August 16). Dozens of Plagiarism incidents Are Reported in Coursera's Free Online Courses. Retrieved from http://chronicle.com/article/dozens-of-plagiarism-incidents/133697/

Young, J. (2012, December 4). Providers of Free MOOCs Now Charge Employers for Access to Student Data. Retrieved from http://chronicle.com/article/providers-of-free-moocs-now/136117/

Young, J. R. (2012). MOOCs Take A Major Step toward Qualifying for College Credit. Chronicle of Higher Education, 59(13), A23.

Young, J. R. (2013, January 15). California State U. Will Experiment With offering Credit for MOOCs. Retrieved February 1, 2013, From The Chronicle of Higher Education: http://chronicle.com/article/california-state-u-will/136677/

Zahn, A., (2013). The Year of The MOOC: How One Weird Acronym Can Help You Get into Your Dream College. C2 Education Be Smarter. Retrieved from http://www.c2educate.com/blog-2/the-year-of-the-mooc-how-one-weird-acronym-can-help-you-get-into-your-dream-college/

INDEX

adaptive learning 35

Big data......................34

Blackmon, S..... 75, 128

Brooks, David 129

Carr, Nicholas .. 22, 25, 28, 32, 34, 35, 36, 38, 129

certificates 7, 16, 85, 86, 88

Cheating 101, 102, 127, 130, 141, 142

Christensen, Clayton 25, 26, 30, 32, 45, 129

Collaboration............57

Connectivism...... 2, 73, 133, 141

Cormier, Dave............2

Coursera . 3, 36, 38, 40, 45, 55, 56, 71, 79, 80, 88, 96, 103, 105, 106, 108, 114, 123, 130, 135, 141, 142, 143

culture 21, 71, 73, 98

Data Mining 34

debundling..........39, 40

disruptive innovation 4, 5, 6, 19, 22, 25, 26, 46, 120, 124

Diversity 57, 71, 73, 133

Educause .. 37, 99, 130, 131, 136

edX 3, 79, 104

effectiveness.............. 92

Friedman, Thomas . 72, 131

Graham, Greg... 34, 36, 41, 132

higher-education budgets 81

Horizon Report....... 33, 136

interaction 6, 10, 11, 13, 42, 47, 48, 49, 50, 51, 52, 53, 56, 57, 58, 59, 60, 65, 68, 74, 114, 120, 121, 136, 139

Interactive 53

Koller, Daphne........ 36

Kolowich, S..... 79, 105, 124, 133

Kuntz, David 35, 36

Lewin, T. 113, 115, 120, 134

Maslow, A. 55, 135

MOOC

   concerns 91

   definition 2

   disruptive innovation 22

   interactivity 47

motivation .. 13, 31, 58, 70, 83, 94, 99, 122

Online Education ... 51, 59, 133, 134, 136

Open Learning Initiative 33

participation 60, 68, 69, 85, 98, 105, 121

peer grading 95, 96, 97, 110

plagiarizing.... 102, 103, 110

Readiness 99

Rees, R 39, 40, 138

remedial.. 116, 117, 123

Samuels, B . 39, 84, 139

self-directed learning 68

Shirky, Clay 45

Snyder, M 76, 81, 91, 102, 140

Social media 9

Thornburg, David...27, 29

Thrun, Sabastian 3, 30, 34, 80, 95, 114, 117

Udacity.....3, 34, 45, 79, 80, 104, 114, 116

Vygotsky 73, 74, 135

Weissmann, J....24, 142

Yirka, B 48, 142

Young, J 117

Zahn, A.............82, 143

Made in the USA
Charleston, SC
22 April 2013